COLLABORATIVE LEARNING

COLLABORATIVE LEARNING

by Edwin Mason

Foreword by Ronald Gross

AGATHON PRESS, INC. ▪ NEW YORK ▪ 1972

Agathon Press, Inc.
150 Fifth Avenue, New York, N.Y. 10011

Library of Congress Catalog Card Number: 72-166549
ISBN Number: 0-87586-028-1

Published by arrangement with Ward Lock Educational
Company Limited

Printed in the United States of America

Contents

Foreword

The book you hold in your hands is, I believe, a uniquely humane, practical, intelligent, and socially relevant vision of what is wrong with secondary education and what should be done about it.

In his Introduction Edwin Mason tells how the book came to be written, and what he is trying to do. My only purpose is to connect some of his perceptions, criticisms, and suggestions to our efforts at radical reform in American secondary education.

I believe that Mason's book, although written from the perspective of an Englishman, is not only consonant with the writing and action that have begun in this country in the past five years, but also a distinct contribution to and advancement of the movement here. "We all live in the same world," he writes early on. We share that world with him not only because it is defined in its public aspect by the same historical and cultural crises, but because of the personal situation we share as teachers:

> To work in a school day after day and feel that we are doing more harm than good, and that with the best will in the world, is too much to bear. But this is what I feel is happening in our secondary schools. The present system is

damaging to most of the people who are caught up in it, adult and young alike. I also feel that although we may not be able to do much about other damaging processes in the overall social system, the situation in schools at least can be remedied if the people working in them will decide to alter the system and effect that decision.

Faced by a comparable conviction, many teachers and educational critics in this country recently have come to similar conclusions. John Holt, Paul Goodman, Herbert Kohl, Peter Marin, Jonathan Kozol, Edgar Friedenberg, George Dennison, George Leonard and others have developed a devastating critique of prevailing practices and begun to articulate genuine alternatives.

As critics, these writers have pointed out that the crisis in American education goes beyond issues of underfinancing, poorly trained teachers, outdated curricula. To them, our schools don't merely fail to achieve their stated purposes. Rather, they argue, many of them are not even decent places for our children to be. Too many schools damage, thwart, stifle children's natural capacity to learn and to grow healthily.

True learning and healthy growth are sabotaged in most American schools today, these critics argue, because of an authoritarian atmosphere in which the emphasis is on the teacher teaching rather than on the student learning. The whole process of schooling is frozen into a rigid lockstep through the grades, chopped up mechanically into blocks of time and different subjects, dominated by a curriculum fixed in advance and imposed from above. There is no real regard for the students as individual people, with real concerns of their own and inherent drives to know, understand, and create.

For John Holt, "To a very great degree, school is a place where children learn to be stupid." Paul Goodman "would not give a penny to the present administrators, and would largely dismantle the present school machinery." The high-school students who formed the Montgomery County (Maryland) Student Alliance testified that "From what we know to be true as full-time students . . . it is quite safe to say that the public schools have critically negative and absolutely destructive effects on human beings and their curiosity, natural desire to learn, confidence, individuality, creativity, freedom of thought and self-respect."

High school education has been a particular target of the radical reformers, and for good reason. High school is the most absurd part of an educational system pervaded by absurdity.

In elementary school, children clearly need some adult supervision to protect them from present dangers. In higher education young adults usually have enough freedom so that they can, if they choose, experiment and enjoy the pleasures and prospects of life. But high school . . .

The students are old enough to take care of themselves, old enough to reject the illegitimate authority of adults, old enough to love and fight and truly learn. To see these formidable creatures docilely submit to the indignities and boredom of the average high school is intolerably sad.

Fortunately, we are increasingly spared that depressant. The students have ceased their acquiescence in the system. The majority of all American high schools have experienced serious disruptions over the past several years—including two-thirds of those in the big cities.

The radical critics and teachers—and, increasingly, the students themselves—have articulated the causes of unrest. As Edgar Friedenberg puts it, "What is learned in high school depends far less on what is taught than on what one actually experiences in the place." And in high school students experience control, mistrust, and punishment. They have little privacy, little free time, little decision-making power. And, of course, they are forced to be there. In this way the schools succeed in teaching conformity, equation of power with legitimate authority, and a deficient sense of respect for dignity and privacy. Inculcation of these values is a major purpose of the schools, and they succeed all too well at it. As Kurt Vonnegut, Jr., has written:

> When you get to be our age, you all of a sudden realize
> that you are being ruled by people you went to high

school with. You all of a sudden catch on that life is nothing *but* high school . . . class officers, cheerleaders, and all . . . . High school is closer to the core of American experience than anything else I can think of.

Boredom, irrelevant curricula, uninspired teaching, and rigid authoritarianism, then, pervade our high schools. These are usually at the heart of student protest and educational criticism. Pressing further, to ask why society has created such institutions, leads to a deeper level of analysis. Schools are designed for distinctively adult needs—social stratification and socialization—and their inhumanity and destructiveness are really by-products of these purposes.

Mason's diagnosis is in accord with all of this. But his affinity with the American radical reformers goes far deeper than agreement about diagnosis. In arguing that the issue of identity is basic, he shares the passion with which Edgar Friedenberg and Peter Marin affirm "the dignity of youth." In demanding a collaborative rather than a competitive environment for learning, he aligns himself with George Leonard and Herbert Kohl. In seeking social relevance in the curriculum, he echoes students throughout the country and writers like Neil Postman and Charles Weingartner who demand that youthful energies be harnessed to making a better society. In insisting that "authenticity of knowledge depends on authenticity of relationship" he joins George Dennison and Paul Goodman and John Holt and James Herndon.

On the face of it, the logical position of radical educators might be to abolish high-school education and to set the kids free. Some do take this position. But a more widespread and influential development has been the creation of new schools which seek to fit education to the kids' needs, not the other way around. After all, young people do need help in growing up, and decent schools can play a major role. Harnessed properly, what George Dennison has called "the natural authority of adults" can benefit youth. What is crucial, however, is to make sure that the schools serve the real needs of students. From this principle it follows that the schools should

4

have curricula that grow out of student interests, that students should play a central role in running the schools, that arbitrary regulations should be abolished, that free and critical thinking should be encouraged, that the pressures of grades, exams, etc., should be ended. In short, the schools should unleash the spirits and impulses of the young, not dam them.

Only in the past several years have high schools in the U.S. moved, even tentatively, in these directions. (Charles Silberman describes some of the pioneering schools in his Carnegie-sponsored survey, *Crisis in the Classroom*.) One thinks of John Adams High School in Portland, Herbert Kohl's Other Ways School in Berkeley, Murray Road in Newton, the "schools without walls" in Philadelphia and Chicago, the LEAP School on New York's lower east side. And, further outside the mainstream of American education, there are numerous Free Schools in which kids and teachers relate to each other in full, generous, authentic ways. Also, there are the Black-initiated experiments, like Harlem Prep, which usually have been based on a collaborative ethos and a rejection of the reduction of the young person to a "student as Nigger" which desiccates most secondary schooling.

Mason offers us a vision of where we might go from here. As his minimal program for change, he would have us radically change the rigid system of testing and grading, the authoritarian structure of the school administration and the classroom, and the organization of the curriculum around subject-matter classes dominated by teachers and organized in a tight timetable. He would have us discard entirely all regular internal school exams, the class as the basic instructional unit, the tracking of students "according to ability," and the conventional class schedule and all the ghastly paraphernalia that support it (bells, traffic rules, Delany cards, etc.) All of this, of course, has been urged for years by secondary educators who are far from radical: J. Lloyd Trump on behalf of the National Association of Secondary School Principals, Ole Sand speaking for the Center for the Study of Instruction of the National Education Association, and esteemed educators like Charles Brown, Lloyd Michael, Alvin Eurich, and Harold Gores.

Collaborative Learning

Mason sees that may of the approaches advocated by previous critics are insufficiently radical. He discerns, for example, that most of the "new curricula" produced by national projects here did not transform the schools because they did not change the relationship between the students and the teachers, nor affect the climate of the schools which so determines the youngsters' attitudes toward learning.

But what makes Mason's book unique is his precise and passionate vision of a new kind of learning and teaching. His unifying concept is that learning is collaborative, and that the center of the high school curriculum should be a kind of "interdisciplinary inquiry" far profounder than the intermixing of conventional subjects so familiar today.

While Mason resists defining his key concept in so many words, for fear of limiting its resonance, he gives various glimpses of its meanings throughout. Learning should be collaborative *between students*, who need each other's perceptions, companionship, and energy for maximum learning. It should be collaborative *between students and teachers*, otherwise it breeds alienation and stifles real achievement. It should be collaborative *with the entire world of knowledge, culture, and experience*, rather than with the slim trickle which is allowed to enter most classrooms.*

These are, of course, the kinds of collaboration through which some of us manage to continue learning *after* graduation. They are merely the ways real people learn in the real world: from each other, from experts with a special skill to teach, from experience and media. But in conventional schools, Mason points out, we do our best to stifle them all. We shut out the stream of information and stimulation from the real world. We isolate students by pitting them against each other competitively, and imposing on them a fierce decorum of silence and regimentation. We cut off communication between students and teachers by confining each to narrow, hierarchic roles. Who could learn in such a place? Who, for that matter, could survive

*Another, closely related view of the concept is given by Mason's colleague, Charity James, in her book *Young Lives at Stake,* Agathon Press, Inc., 1972—R.G.

there? (I'm reminded of a question Staughton Lynd asks in an unpublished paper on "The New Academician": "Who can remember a teacher who began the year by saying: 'Here is a problem for us to solve together?' ")

Even in our most radically experimental "free schools," we often find a mirror image of this society's excessive individualism. "Do-your-own-thing" replaces the scramble for grades. But these schools still lack those intense rewards which come only, or most readily, from cooperative achievement: shared insights, accidental joys, a sense of community.

The scope of Mason's concept of collaborative learning is indicated in several places in the book, each illuminating it from a different angle. A superb summary statement suggests the learning and teaching styles implied by the concept:

> Major questions or problems of concern to the youngster should be located and explored in small collaborative groups. Teachers should act as advisers, not directors, offering the benefits of their mature common sense as well as their specialist expertise, and helping to put the youngsters in touch with other people or resources demanded by the progress of the enquiry. They should especially try to help by offering methodological advice and criticism enabling the youngsters to become more aware of the processes of hypothesis and prediction they are using. Teachers should also sensitize themselves to deeper observation of the collaborative interaction within the small groups and between groups. A small group or cluster of children occasionally collaborating with another cluster is to be preferred to a large group, even where both groups are largely duplicating the same work. Effective collaboration without clear division of labor falls off rapidly as group size grows beyond five members.

The range of activities used for learning and teaching is as wide as one can imagine:

> There are many techniques through which the enquiring mind realizes its world. All of these should be regarded as

appropriate and the whole range encouraged to develop without a preference for written work of the kind now called for most frequently in school. Role playing, other kinds of simulation, invention of games, controlled experiments, experiments in observation, sensual exercises, studies in perception and interpersonal perception, modelling, all kinds of making, all of which takes place amidst continual discussion of what they are doing among the youngsters themselves, is to be aimed for.

No constraints are to be placed on the inquiring mind:

There should ideally be no restrictions of subject matter or of modes of discovery, problem solving, experiment or study used in interdisciplinary enquiry. It should not be confined by fashionable preferences in academic method. All media should be used and entirely practical work be welcomed.

And, finally, the natural transition of knowledge into action is stressed:

The call is clearly for enquiry, not for integrated studies, and for opportunities to *do* something, to explore powers of action, as well as for verbal speculation. The young can be dispassionate and reasonable enough but they cannot be impersonal, nor can the learning they are seeking be encompassed without action. It is not merely more initiative in deciding on topics to study in school that interdisciplinary enquiry should allow for. The way into adult life for the adolescent is through ruminative speculation, shared with a few of his fellows, leading to visions of possible courses of action. Frustrate the action and you frustrate the true intellectual developments for which the adolescent is ready and which are likely to wither in the bud if the season of that readiness is missed.

This central concept of Mason's is very potent. Learning is in *fact* collaborative where it is authentic and effective; it *must* and *should* be collaborative if we wish it to achieve authenticity and effectiveness; and it *can* be collaborative if we change our ways of running our schools. The exploration of the concept's ramifications will be the work of many hands, many minds. I think it is a vastly promising new perspective for secondary schooling—and for achieving a more human life of learning outside of schools.

For Mason knows that true educational reform implies changing far more than schools—even if the school changes envisaged are fundamental indeed. He never loses sight of the fact that the real point of our efforts at school reform is to abet the birth of a new man and a new society.

The kind of man and society to which the author aspires is the radically humanist one of Ivan Illich, Erich Fromm, and Danilo Dolci. He envisages man re-unified, reconstituted in his full dignity and in his direct engagement with experience, man free to exercise the full range of his powers: intellectual, emotional, intuitive, and political.

His ideal society, similarly, is one of institutions and associations that are voluntary, convivial, and creative, rather than coercive and manipulative, bureaucratic and reductive, authoritarian and rigid.

These images of man and society yield his images of the student and the school. Only a student who learns in a school run like that society, can become that kind of man. A humane school is the necessary, though not the sufficient, cradle of a truly human man and a truly humane society.

Collaborative learning, then, is not merely the name of a new pedagogical program. Rather, and more importantly, it signifies a life-style which Mason sums up in a paraphrase of the Beatles' line: "We can all get by with (maybe more than a little) help from our friends." For those committed to educational and social reform in this country, Edwin Mason is a friend who gives us, in this book, no little help.

Ronald Gross, *July, 1971*
co-editor, with Beatrice Gross,
of *Radical School Reform*
(Simon & Schuster, 1970) and, with
Paul Osterman, of *High School*
(Simon & Schuster, 1971)

To Jonathan and all his generation

i am fifteen years old

somebody
is trying to
make me
add up

when all that i
want to do
is multiply

Introduction
and Acknowledgments

Honesty compels me to begin this book with a careful and lengthy identification of the point of view from which it will be written. Through years of reading away at the literature of educational discussion (feeling more often than not like a mouse nibbling at the foothills of a mountain range) I have myself come to be mistrustful of anything that pretends to impersonality. When we make any kind of educational decision, we are determining to do something with somebody else's life. The reformer has a clear responsibility at least to show his hand and explain how he comes to be holding the cards he intends to play, for there is no authority to turn to and in this book there will be no appeal anywhere to research findings or to custom.

My point of view is one I share with many people, most of whom I have never met or worked with. It is one shared by very many teachers, as my extensive contact with teachers over the last few years has shown me. Still they may be startled by what I have to say in this book, especially by the urgency with which I feel we need to change our ways and the extent to which I think we must change them.

To work in a school day after day and feel that we are doing more harm than good, and that with the best will in the world, is too much to bear. But this is what I feel is happening in our secondary schools. The present system is damaging to most of the people who are caught up in it, adult and young alike. I also feel that although we may not be able to do much about other damaging processes in the overall social system, the situation in schools at least can be remedied if the people working in them will decide to alter the system and effect that decision. Much of this book will explain how that can be done.

But we are not likely even to begin until we realize that

> our ingenuity in devising alternative constructions is limited by our feeble wits and our timid reliance upon what is familiar. So we usually do things the way we have done them before or the way others appear to do them. Moreover novel ideas, when openly expressed, can be disruptive to ourselves and disturbing to others. We therefore often avoid them, disguise them, keep them bottled up in our minds where they cannot develop in a social context, or disavow them in what we believe to be loyalty to the common interest. And often, against our better judgment, we accept the dictates of authority instead, thinking thus to escape any personal responsibility for what happens.
>
> But . . . it does not follow that facts ever dictate our conclusions, except by the rules we impose upon our acts. Events do not tell us what to do, nor do they carry their meanings engraved on their backs for us to discover. For better or worse we ourselves create the only meanings they will convey during our lifetime . . . Our ever present task is to devise ways of anticipating their occurrences, and thus to prepare ourselves for assuming a more and more responsible role in the management of the universe.[1]

I am concerned to examine the rules we impose on our acts as teachers. In accepting them we impose other rules on the young, rules which I think actually prevent them from learning and certainly prevent them from assuming "a responsible role in the management of the universe."

Introduction and Acknowledgments

To find the personal origins of my point of view I would have to go back into my mother's lifetime. The origins of this book do not demand quite such a long search. I have only to go back eight years, to the time when I resigned from the post of deputy headmaster of a London comprehensive school specifically to begin work on a complete, personal revaluation of the secondary curriculum. I did not know how I was going to set about it (except that ideas I had already explored such as "integration of subjects" didn't look very promising) and I didn't know where to find allies. But I did have a conviction, which had grown for years and which the opportunity of administering a comprehensive school had done nothing to allay, that our secondary schools were meeting neither the needs of the young nor the demands of the world; that the steps we were taking to reform them were too piecemeal, random and timid; that they might even be steps in the wrong direction.

That conviction has grown even stronger over the years in which I have been able to examine our educational system minutely. So also has the underlying conviction which drives me and emerges in the heat with which I write this book, the conviction that unless somehow soon human arrogance can be tamed and human social incompetence remedied, humanity and maybe even the human species will disappear. For of all creatures on earth, we are the least competent to survive. We are the species most at risk because we are the species which is its own enemy. Other species do not need to make the effort to understand themselves or invent ways of understanding to replace old ways that obviously didn't work but which remain as entrenched perceptual habits. We do. Other species have not broken the bounds of their nature. We have.

This problem can no longer be deferred; neither can the problem of educational reform. Our generation's bequest to its children is a vast wealth of technological power. The rest of the inheritance is a ruined environment, much of it irreparably damaged, and a society that has no system of controlling its own destructive power collectively or individually.

The dangers I am talking of are many. I am not merely referring to the familiar fear we all have of a final war between

13

the super nations—Armageddon post-Hiroshima style. I fear equally what has happened in Vietnam, what will happen in Latin America; the massacres whch recur in Indonesia and Malaysia and Africa, and the reinstitution of superstitious totalitarian regimes as in Greece and Czechoslovakia. The world is in a state of endless roaming war. Tyrannies hold life cheap. So in their own way do bureaucracies. And as the weapons in the hands of the police and their masters in police states become ever subtler and more efficient, it is harder to hide from them in order to muster resistance and easier for them to manipulate information to rouse public support. It becomes harder to fight them without coming to hold life as cheap as they do. The tragedy of Ché Guevara is not so much that he died but that he became in the end the prisoner of ideology rather than the servant of more sweeping and vaguer ideals; that even in him (and he was a man of genuinely heroic stature) the true inner voice of values was edged out by the internalized crudities of the mass media version of his original message. These efficient tyrannies will not be ended except by force unless a genuine international system of collective support for human rights which ignores national boundaries can be established. But the present United Nations is even further from this ideal than the old League. The world is becoming more, not less, nationalistic. International affairs is a matter of government-of-a-nation speaking unto government-of-a-nation.

And the weapons of all these wars? They are no less terrifying than the fusion bomb. Tyrannies use lies and fear founded on what everybody knows happens in the backrooms of the local police station but can't be proved in an international court until the regime is overthrown and its own careful records become available. In civil war the weapons become more and more readily those of international war, and in international war the weapons are lies again, ideology, fire in chemical jellies, disturbers of the ecological balance which make great tracts of land useless, destroying the result of hundreds of years of human care overnight; and virtually any biochemical weapon the military technocrats (served by utterly irresponsible members of the faculties of reputable universities) care to experiment with; and the universities receive subsidies for the work and "secret" government classification to suppress public knowledge of what is going on.

Nowhere in the world, it seems, do we admit wise men to government—wisdom admits the realities of death and pain, offers no cheerful excuses for the human condition but maintains a reverence for life, and not only for human life either. Nowhere in the world is there any effective collective control of public policy, nor a common level of literacy capable of dealing with the semantic confusion which is now the main tool of government control. Even the governors, men of little wisdom, fall for their own propaganda. It is only too likely that Papadopoulos is stupid enough to believe he is defending Christendom and rebuilding Byzantium and Nixon obviously believes Americans are free.

And if there is no collective control, who is to stop our interference with nature? There is always a lobby somewhere defending somebody's right to profit from the invention and exploitation of destructive drugs, chemicals or machines, or from building another dam to provide more cheap electric power with which to industrialize yet another area of the globe, or from building city centres consisting only of rented office and shop accommodation, or from pouring through the rivers into the oceans enough poisons to alter the whole environment in ten years. The Pacific is vast but there are no more sardines to be caught off the Californian coast, while the lives of inhabitants of Pacific islands are actually threatened by a once rare poisonous jellyfish. To be powerless to prevent all this, should by chance you ever be aware it is happening, is even more frightening than to have no control over your government's foreign policy or over your town planners. Furthermore you are drenched by propaganda in the form both of commercial advertising for such products and an imbued sense of reverence for affluence founded on their existence and proliferation, and of a value system that esteems science not because science is a highly skilful kind of curiosity but because it gives us all these weapons, all this power.

Most frightening of all to me (and the reason why this book

takes the form it does, nagging away at the problem of identity) is how this information environment reinforces the alienation of people by making it less likely that they can know what to demand of life in the way of collective control of human action. A true community is a community of odd people, not a regiment of men selected because they are so alike it is hard to tell one from another. The only reliable kind of selfesteem enjoys our own uniqueness and seeks to know and enjoy everybody else's too. It can only grow where we *do* have power to contribute our unique personal vision and personal skill to the community.

In authoritarian ant hills, this opportunity to make personal gifts is suspect; it is after all a bid for power. But the bids for power we make are not initially antisocial. They are, in that they represent what we can do and *give*, the very basis of society. If education is to be a process which maintains the momentum of society, it *must* be a process which enables people to give what they have. It must in individual terms be an identity building process. This explains why throughout this book I use the effects of the educational system on identity as my measure of its worth. All the business about the nature of disciplines or subjects as constellations of information hanging together in characteristic ways, which I find most teachers want to talk about first and which looms larger in educational literature than anything else, is secondary and I have relegated it to the position it merits. It is only important as a tool of identity.

Becker[2] puts the first priority more simply than I have:

> Selfesteem becomes the child's feeling of selfwarmth that it's all right in his action world. Thus, the seemingly trite words 'selfesteem' are at the very core of human adaptation.

And elsewhere:

> Action that meets satisfaction gives the nascent ego a feeling of mastery. Selfidentity, in simplest terms, is basically the experience of executive control of one's own powers of action. Since the ego grows by learning

techniques for controlling anxiety—repression, denial, and so on—the identity of the child is built on a growing sense of mastery. As the ego solves the problem of anxiety, it also learns the pleasures of anxiety-free mastery.

Note that it is not mastery of *others* we set out to seek. It is mastery of our own powers of action. If this is frustrated by others who see our bid as a bid for control of *them*, who think of all mastery as mastery of each other, it will inevitably happen that we cast our search in those terms too and that we will become locked in a situation of rivalry we will never resolve. Instead of collaborating with others to extend our mastery of our own action as our nature bids us, our repertoire of everything but immediate personal competition strategy will dwindle instead of grow in this situation. Many become convinced that they are born losers, very many more come to think of themselves as born passengers; few come to see the whole field of human learning as their proper *Lebensraum* or playground.

How can we eliminate this energy-sapping rivalry and produce a system of schooling which encourages collaboration for everybody's sake? That is the question I mean to explore in this book. Since it runs so directly against the tide of working values, if not of face values of our society, where private enterprise is seen as bargaining for privileges and in no sense the giving of gifts, I do not expect a ready initial agreement that the question is even important. Hence my first three chapters. As the secretary of the Association of Approved School Headmasters said, supporting Alec Dickson's scheme for organizing the release of approved school inmates into the kind of community service projects many secondary schools undertake, "This has been regarded by some as a terribly sophisticated concept." The concept is Dickson's: "This is the first time some young people who have felt rejected for most of their lives are having the opportunity to give something. I believe that this giving part is the missing dimension in their rehabilitation."[3]

It may seem even more sophisticated of me to suggest that the opportunity to prove yourself capable of giving others is the opportunity actually to have a self and not a matter of rehabilitation at all. To *give*, I mean, not to bargain for the right to be a member of society. The idea has not yet sunk in that society is common property, membership in which comes with birth and does not have to be earned. Or is this suggestion another piece of egalitarian nonsense? Face and working values contradict each other here. Children born in Wolverhampton of Indian, West Indian or African parents or even grandparents are commonly referred to as immigrants there today. Gypsies whose families may have lived in England for centuries are being harassed with increasing violence and set upon by thugs from "security firms" employed by local councils. And to be noticeably poor, or to be loudmouthed and insistently impolite about the lies told in our society about its condition will very soon attract the comment that you are in some way "inadequate." Inadequate for what? It may very well mean "inadequate to take the education offered on condition that it shall be of a kind appropriate to those who have a proved capacity to compete for it."

The conclusions expressed by J. B. Mays summarizing Dr. Crawford's investigations into some Liverpool schools seem to me even more significant than he himself indicates:

> Clearly all the children in the neighbourhoods which did badly academically suffered from a cultural impoverishment, a general absence of parental support and consequent lack of motivation towards high achievement in school. . . . It is also clear that the schools they attended . . . contributed further debilitating influences which in combination with the shortcomings of the local milieu . . . tended to create and perpetuate a tradition of inertia and a pattern of typical underprivilege. The pupils in these schools were on the whole being prepared for second or even third class citizenship.[4]

This sort of thinking, given that it is quite true of the relative positions of those we punish and those we reward, enables those of us who are not obviously being excluded, those of us who feel that we have somehow earned membership of the club, always to see the inadequacy in somebody else or in some distant sector of the system. But if the society itself is third rate, will it have any first-rate citizens? Society after all is *not* a club, nor even a mere association or federation of clubs. We cannot claim it is healthy while exclusiveness is so prominent a feature of its discipline, or while the punitive impulse is given such free play. It is the "traditions of inertia and patterns of typical underprivilege" of our society as a whole expressed in the organization of *most* of our social systems, and perhaps especially in our educational system, that we should be worrying about. Our haste to apply special remedies to people unlike us with no aim other than to make them *like* us (the ambiguity is intended) is not the least worrying manifestation of the human arrogance I revealed my fear of earlier. To feel like that about other people is indeed to be inadequate to the demands of the world as it is—a world which has a future that cannot be deferred, a world in which now live a fifth of all the people who have ever lived, a world which contains a fifth of all the creative human power there has ever been, but very much more than a fifth of the historical total of destructive human power. The hard-edged, crustacean kind of self that goes with a basically exclusive society, the self that has been taught to reject, reject and reject again, to scratch until it itches, to mistake introspection for insight, is the genuine inadequate in such a world. The inadequacy of the tout for such a society is as bad as the inadequacy of the lout he despises.

Perhaps I am adopting too hectoring a tone. After all, I have been damaged too and to become aware of that is only a beginning. I wish I had the strength of direct vision Danilo Dolci has and I turn to him without making any excuses that I live in a country where the issues are less clear cut, because that is not the case—we all live in the same world:

On the magnificent beach of the Bay of Castellammare . . . a woman is lighting a little fire down near the edge of the water and laying out on a grill a row of freshly caught red mullet, while her family play about in the sea and the sun. A number of youths—some of whom are in fact qualified teachers—happen to be hanging around nearby and they start muttering: "Really! What a disgrace! What a way to

19

behave! How can anyone still do things like that? *Decent* people would go to a restaurant" and so on, making fun of her, their voices getting louder and louder. And yet these same young men apparently see nothing immoral in continuing to serve as touts at election time for a local candidate who is notoriously well disposed towards the Mafia, in the hope that he will pull strings for them in return and get them fixed up with jobs.[5]

The Mafia, I remind myself, doesn't call itself the Mafia but "The Honorable Society."

I wish, with gratitude, to use more of his insight from the same magnificent book *For the Young*, commenting only that it is high time we stopped treating Dolci with the kind of reverence accorded saints, who are to be respected but not imitated, and started to see him as the sound, realistic social, political and educational theorist he is.

Measured against the following quotation, for instance, what are we to say of those 1,200 days which are the least our children spend in school, days of leapfrogging from topic to topic?

None of us can develop properly unless we are allowed opportunities for concentration and creative thinking and unless we establish a new attitude towards each other and towards the world itself. It is only too easy for the process of natural curiosity and learning through direct experience to be obstructed, instead of being encouraged and develop-ed as it should be. And so, as a person grows up, his understanding of the world comes to be based on a vast mass of unconnected acts of faith, concerning both trivial and fundamental questions, all jumbled up in his mind with little fragments of his own experience. It is not surprising, then, if after a while he begins to take it for granted that he is quite incapable of ever coordinating his vision of life into an organic whole.

Too many people as they grow up allow their attention and their interests to be limited and restricted to an insane degree. Nowadays, the number of people who still have a direct and basic relationship with the real world is getting smaller and smaller; the artist, perhaps, and the scientist, and the peasant, and the fisherman—but how open and free is even *their* relationship?[6]

There is no nostalgia for childhood here; and clearly none of the nostalgia of which Dr. Leavis has been accused in his years of arguing our desperate need of an organic society, from his early pamphlet *Mass Civilization and Minority Culture* onwards. What most distinguishes Leavis as a critic from those who try to whittle yardsticks for measuring literature is the fact that his literary criticism is also social criticism, that his search is for something that Dolci is also expressing, in his terms: how men come to "realize" their world and life with language which is not only common social property but a living product of human collaboration. Realities are made, not found, and authenticity of knowledge depends on authenticity of relationship—a phrase I owe to Lévi-Strauss and explore at greater length later.

At this point I have arrived at a major difficulty which I shall not try to overcome here. I am not going to try to tell you what this book means. I propose to offer a summary at the end of each chapter, but that is only to emphasize *some* of the points I make on the way. They are not definitions nor are they route maps. My thinking is not linear and I do not seek definitions, which in their pretense to finality seem to me the most treacherous of all possible uses of language.

My objections to subject teaching for instance are threefold. First I object because school days timetabled that way reduce the day to a succession of trivialities by excluding fundamental questions since they can never be confined within any subject, and even to make a broad science/humanities division is bound to exclude some discipline which should be contributing to the exploration. Second, far more subjects are needed than can ever be included *as subjects*. Anthropology taught by a history specialist who sees what he is doing as teaching history will be very peculiar anthropology. His aim should be to advise the young on where to look for evidence available from both disciplines, admitting that he is a poor anthropologist but at

21

least avoiding the temptation to distort anthropology. Third, there is an inbuilt danger of overdefinitiveness in specialist teaching, originating in the difficulty of selecting evidence to examine which will encourage the slow acquisition of the discipline of the subject rather than deteriorate into the teaching of facts (by which I mean necessarily inauthentic, nonrealized knowledge—what Dolci calls "acts of faith" in the teacher). To know authentically is to know tentatively. The claim of definition is the claim to be in known territory where questions are closed. We should encourage an attitude towards verbal definitions like that of the mathematician towards infinity, which he regards not as the point at which things go on repeating themselves for ever in exactly the same way, but rather as the point at which he gives up, recognizing that he has gone as far as we know to a point where things are beyond what we know.

So it is not merely for fear of being quoted in examination scripts that I offer no definition of collaborative learning anywhere in this book. My use of the term throughout is an expression of my repudiation of all theories of learning founded on observation of what people do in closed system situations arbitrarily set up to observe learning events. This repudiation extends to schools, since they also are highly arbitrary closed systems in which the only observations made are of learning events called lessons. What I am offering by insisting that learning can be understood only if collaboration can be understood, is an invitation to declare a moratorium on the development and application of learning theories while we explore collaborations instead and see whether better learning results from the change of approach. I cannot think of any part or moment of life in which we are not reacting to the presence of other people, or carrying over into relationship with everything else, what we have learned (by no means all of it consciously) from collaborating with other people while exploring the world with them. It is not only to move mountains that men collaborate; we collaborate to pass the time pleasantly and, if we make love well, to make love, and it does not exclude conflict. "Collaboration may take the form of disagreement and one is grateful to the critic whom one has found worth disagreeing with."[7]

This book owes its existence to my luck in being in the right place at the right time to help institute, in collaboration with teachers, an experiment sufficiently long term to escape being a mere learning event. The opportunity for me, and the beginning of the first curriculum laboratory of its kind in Britain, came from the decision to continue in-service courses for experienced secondary school teachers to explore the curriculum of secondary schools, following the great success of such a course mounted by Goldsmiths' College at the behest of the Department of Education and Science, and directed by Charity James (who has published her own plea for change)[8] and Professor Gene Philips of Boston University in the spring of 1965. This course had both the warm support and the participation of the Warden of Goldsmiths' College, Dr. Chesterman, who has supported our work throughout, not as an administrator finding house room for a strange pet, but as a teacher taking a direct, personal critical interest in all the issues we have become embroiled in, as indeed have many colleagues in all the faculties of Goldsmiths' College who have willingly consulted with members of the courses we run.

The first group, which included many headteachers, needed no prompting to repudiate its terms of reference—a curriculum for children of average and less than average ability, aged thirteen to sixteen—but insisted that they should explore the nature of secondary schools as a whole. They produced as a handout for a conference to declare their findings at the end of the eleven-week course, a lengthy report which left no question unasked and no resentment at what our schools do to youngsters and teachers alike unexpressed. As a thoroughly thrashed-out open-minded statement collaboratively produced by a group of experienced teachers and educationists, it is a genuinely revolutionary document. It even has the temerity and the goodwill to include A Bill of Rights for Adolescents which goes well beyond the demands now being made by a new union of schoolchildren which is trying to find its feet.

It also established a working pattern which we decided to

adopt with all groups of teachers we worked with: that the group should eventually produce a report of the areas covered, much of which might be derived from working papers submitted as we went along by smaller groups who had decided to explore some more narrow issue. The final reports were prepared for publication by me and I aimed only to include what was agreed by consensus, contributing quite heavily myself especially on matters which had been thoroughly discussed by the group but not written up as working papers. Demand for copies of the first group's report was so great that the stencils fell to pieces. I re-edited it immediately after editing the second group's report and it has been reprinted since several times, as have all the six reports published as an outcome of seven courses. The only other requirement imposed on members of courses has been that they should give some time to practicing an art, preferably one they have not tried before. Apart from these fixtures there has been no preliminary structuring of the courses by the tutors.

The result of this decision to hold fast to democracy was initially difficult for us to carry out genuinely, since most teachers coming on courses ask for direction just as they maintain their pupils do (and even more cheerfully disregard it if it is offered) and we have had to become skilled at resisting the demand. We are all preachers by nature, I think, and it was not easy. I myself often fall into the trap of overdoing the withdrawal and have stayed silent for days on end, only to let nobody else get a word in edgeways on another day. This does no harm and in fact, I think, if I do not allow myself to be as moody as everybody else is allowed to be and fulfil the equality I offer a group when I choose to work in this way, I would seem to be offering to play some professional role of a therapeutic nature for which I am not fitted, and which I think would be a dangerous sign of alienation anyway, as well as being plain impertinence to people many of whom have been teaching quite as long as I have. I shall discuss the implications of this later when I write of the difficulties teachers will meet when working in a reorganized system and relating much more often to small groups than to classes. The stresses are very similar and arise from the fact that, do what you will, while you carry a label which distinguishes you from the group, like tutor or teacher or in my case grandiloquently Director of Courses, the difficulties the group runs into are slightly exaggerated. The root cause of these difficulties is reported by Ottaway in his observations on working with small groups: "In fact people don't speak freely about things that really matter until they feel they can trust the group with what they have to say."[9] Trust the *group* mind you, not just some individuals in it. Nobody trusts a large group. We act as committee men in large groups, not as whole beings. To be selfrevealing demands small group work and somebody around who will take the risk of seeming dotty.

If you form a group for group introspection, you run the risk of having people produce strange self versions to use as counters in bids for the group's attention and affection. Something of this happens anyway, but it is well enough contained if the group has other work to do and if understanding each other is necessary to get something done. This is the situation with our groups, as it is with youngsters in school. Beyond that I wouldn't like to push the parallel between the way we work with teachers in our curriculum laboratory and the way the teachers work with youngsters in schools. We after all are not adults in the making. We are adults learning to let ourselves unwind.

I have got used to the stresses I meet with in these strange meetings. So have my colleagues. Every year until now we have had a visiting American professor to help us and provoke us. We have now added instead to the permanent team an American lady anglicized by marriage, Mrs. Sonya Caston, to whom I'm already heavily indebted for some ideas I'm using here, especially the notion of "expert childhood" as a transitional phase into adolescence.

My debt to all my visiting colleagues can no more be described or disentangled than my debt to the 193 teachers we have worked with so far in courses, the many more we have had contact with in schools or in correspondence, the expert consultants we have been able to call on in our discussions, the architects and the student architects who have especially seemed to find an affinity with us, the social workers who have worked with us, and the educationists who have dropped in from the USA, Canada, Rhodesia, what used to be called the Antipodes, from Malta and from the Transkei, some for only a day, some for as long as four weeks. They are all represented somehow in this book, for they have all been involved in discussing the issues I am reporting in my entirely personal way. None of them is directly quoted but they are all here. I have not even quoted the published reports (though I have drawn heavily in parts on my own contributions to them) but they are here too.

Here most of all are my two closest colleagues and friends, Charity James and Leslie Smith, and much of Sam Mauger who left us to work in industrial relations. On a personal level, though I hope it is written not only for my own sake, this book is a history of my own struggles to escape from the alienation which is our common cultural heritage. If I succeed in this, it will be especially through having worked with Charity, Leslie and our administrative assistant, Mary Darby, who have the courage not to shut their eyes to the world as it is and encourage me to keep mine open.

Since it was Emile Durkheim who first clearly delineated alienation, I shall use his expression of the force which can oppose it, which I find a true expression of my working life with such colleagues:

> When individual minds are not isolated but enter into close relation with and work upon each other, from their synthesis arises a new kind of psychic life. It is clearly distinguished by its peculiar intensity from that led by the solitary individual . . . . It is in a sense a luxurious activity since it is a very rich activity . . . periods of creation or renewal occur when men for various reasons are led into a closer relationship with each other, when . . . relationships are better maintained and the exchange of ideas most active.[10]

It happens best when people come together sharing a common

hope. It happens least when people are restrained from giving. We have great need for it to happen for our young.

Freud also saw in the life of man a struggle of opposing forces which were displaced from society into the individual and referred thence into society again to emerge in violence or violation, or in "the tradition of inertia" which Mays saw in the slums of Liverpool and which I see as a characteristic of our social system. For Freud the opposed forces in the individual issuing in social action were a tendency to repudiate life altogether and a lifewelcoming will, Eros:

> Men have brought their powers of subduing the forces of nature to such a pitch that by using them they could now very easily exterminate one another to the last man. They know this—hence arises a great part of their current unrest, their dejection, their mood of apprehension. And now it may be expected that the other of the two 'heavenly forces,' eternal Eros, will put forth his strength so as to maintain himself alongside of his equally immortal adversary.[11]

This perhaps gives some clues to the only answer I could make to readers who may find the early part of this book gloomy. How can a man who takes such a dark view of the present human condition, who repudiates progress, rejects all the old modes of revolution and most of the old modes of reform, write as if anything could be done to alter our schools?

Fortunately Eros is born unschooled. It is our social systems that are at fault, not the equipment we are born with and this means we are not powerless. It is open to all of us to come to a better understanding of life if we are willing to try and to accept the fact that improvement in our understanding will demand some change in ourselves which we must be prepared to make. Given that we can become more generous to our young, give without bargaining and accept what they have to give us. They need not grow up as meanly as we have.

We can all get by with (maybe more than a little) help from our friends.

27

Collaborative Learning

References

1. G. A. Kelly, quoted in D. Bannister and J. M. M. Mair, *The Evaluation of Personal Constructs* (Academic Press, 1968).
2. Ernest Becker, *The Birth and Death of Meaning* (Free Press of Glencoe 1962; Collier, 1963).
3. *Sunday Times* report, August 17, 1969.
4. J. B. Mays, *The Young Pretenders* (Michael Joseph, 1965; Schocken, 1968).
5. Danilo Dolci, *For the Young* (MacGibbon and Kee, 1967).
6. See note 5 above.
7. F. R. Leavis, *The Common Pursuit* (Chatto and Windus, 1952).
8. Charity James, *Young Lives at Stake* (Collins, 1968; Agathon, 1971).
9. A. K. C. Ottaway, *Learning Through Group Experience* (Routledge, 1966; Humanities Press, 1966).
10. Emile Durkheim, *Essays on Sociology and Philosophy* (Harper and Row, 1965).
11. Sigmund Freud, *Civilization and Its Discontents* (Hogarth Press, 1930; Norton, 1962).

CHAPTER 1
Challenge to Our Educational System

Although at times in this book I shall have to use a few terms for new schooling processes I have helped to define, I want to avoid using the special language of schools and the jargons which proliferate from time to time to contain and confine discussion of education. Though I believe that teachers should be expert, I do not believe that education is a business best left to experts, and the growth of an esoteric experts' language always ends in a take-over bid by some minority. Where bounds are set to confine discussion, educational policies shrink to implementing ploys that can easily be measured and corralled into the care of an individual specialist, and so the deepest of our collective responsibilities is taken out of our hands. It is small wonder that our schools, instead of being foyers leading into the universe of discourse that human life could be, have become sideshows at a trades fair where the young are led to take potshots at knowledge, set out as so many Aunt Sallies, every one labelled. How many times are our youngsters told to "take another shot" at history, maths, or some other subject?

We are left with lamentably unambitious educational policies in a world where the human condition is patently parlous as a direct result of the policies we have so far pursued. The greater our powers, the greater the threat to our survival as beings whose lives are worth living.

The current academic fashion, which I shall not attempt to follow here, is to limit discussion of education severely to the design of short-term programs aimed at achieving clearly defined objectives. The school is to become even more like a behaviorist laboratory. Learning is thought of as a process in which an agent—the teacher—does "the right things" to a client—the student—in a prearranged optimum environment designed for the performance of the operation. I intend to argue that learning is not like that and life should not be. But I cannot pretend to find it strange in a world where surgery is the most prestigious mode of medicine and warfare still the trade which attracts the most investment (space exploration is a military byproduct) that the imagery of the two professions is not only confused, but dominates most human endeavor. The battlefield is a "theatre of operations" where some malignant part of the enemy is your target. To remove an objectionable "ism" (commun- or capital-) we perform an operation. It may be devastating the land; it may be washing the "ism" out of an individual mind. And at this point it becomes difficult to distinguish between military objectives and some educational objectives. Bombard the cancer and the evil will disappear. Bombard the child and defeat the devil. Aversion therapy is a new name for an old process familiar to anyone who ever went to school.

The model provided by the use of the term objectives is easily manageable because we have all been brought up to it and it is part of a paradigm, a whole group of assumptions we are unlikely to question. It belongs with the assumption that it is both desirable and possible to prefabricate the human future. If you reject these assumptions, as I think we now must, you will mistrust the model. It is time to work from something vaguer and stronger, a hope to see our children grow, to seek in a positive and curious way better ways of stabilizing human welfare than we ourselves have achieved. Looking at our world as it is (not at some even more frightful future) I take it to be an impertinence to be talking still of education as a process of passing on our own culture. What in our traditions is still worth preserving is in fact the unpopular part, that which questions all authority. It is however a commonplace impertinence performed daily in all the classrooms of the world, where a set of descriptions is being passed off as reality.

We who are schooling our own and other people's children have been schooled ourselves, and the better schooled we were the harder we find it to understand why anybody should want to change an educational system anyway. We can all see of course that this or that detail may need altering, but why redesign the whole thing from scratch? And even when the system has been redesigned we are likely to prefer a model not unlike the old one. We can always admit to the odd mistake but not to having taken part in an operation radically hostile to life.

At this stage I have to invite the reader to exercise his imagination vigorously and to look anywhere but at schools as they are for an answer to the questions

1. Why does the educational system need thorough redesigning?
2. How can we measure the urgency of the need for change in educational practice or determine its scope?
3. On what grounds (if not those of narrow specific objectives) can educational decisions be made?
4. On how wide a range of deliberations should we base them?

Had we any evidence from anywhere in the world of any old-style social stability we could take our time in answering, but all the evidence points to the fact that the world is in turmoil and consequently more and more of the people in it are in personal turmoil. Even the short-term future, despite the valiant effort of the strange fish in government think tanks charged with the solemn duty of soothsaying, becomes increasingly unpredictable. We know enough about the effects of the whirligig of technological innovation to be staggered by the possibilities but we cannot really tell what they will do to us. In the direct field of human affairs sociology turns out to have failed us by remaining respectably descriptive of what was, and history seems barely relevant. We cannot be sure that any information about what is happening in the world now should be excluded and there seems to be no discipline which has nothing to offer to the argument.

The personal predicament of anyone trying to think about all this is most saliently that we don't know where to turn for information. Too much of it is encoded in ways we have not mastered. We find that we have to rely on others and need to find out how best to work with them. We can neither master all that matters nor do without some understanding of the matters we cannot master. Complete ignorance becomes dangerously threatening because it may indeed imperil our lives and certainly it weakens our identity to be utterly at sea in a foreign universe which becomes daily less familiar as yet another assumption we were reared to take for natural law is dismissed. It is at this level when we find the external turmoil does and must throw us into personal turmoil that it hits us hardest.

And if we find any element of this turmoil within ourselves, we should recognize that it gives us a starting point for assessing how we need to change our ways as educators. We should begin, if we can, to work out what it is that people have to cope with now and may be expected to have to cope with in future in order to form a picture of human needs not in the abstract but in the environment as we perceive it now. We must also, when rethinking the educational system, see the young as young and growing, and examine what demands their own growth make upon them from day to day.

These peculiar needs of youngsters in adolescence I shall discuss in the next chapter. Here I am concerned with a broad and necessarily rather random review of the human problems which seem to me most significant now that the moon is a walked-on rock and not the lamp that comes out of entanglements of fairy tale to chase a child down a side street.

The problems that matter most are those least often discussed which are common to us all, not those which can be earmarked as belonging to any profession. They are the problems of human beings whose need it is to find ways of becoming more fully human and of protecting their enhanced humanity. The foremost demand made by this need is that we find better ways of undertaking collective responsibility for our actions, something more genuinely democratic than the representative democracy which is the face value reading of our normal relationships in a highly functionary division-of-labor economy. We have to identify and attack the working values underlying the face values of normal relationships in our society. It should matter most to us in a world where relationships are increasingly bureaucratized and dehumanized, where we are taught and driven to know each other more by decoding our stigmata than by recognizing our dreams, that we can still learn to know ourselves as human social organisms, and repudiate any account of ourselves as things, items, or machines. We are not cogs. Our life together is not a matter of our rough edges occasionally interlocking. We should then repudiate any social system that reduces our contact to that level and any language model that helps us to accept such impoverishment. This of course means that we must very carefully re-examine what is taught to clear out mechanistic dead wood from all disciplines studied. It would not be difficult to find in all areas, not only of curriculum but of all public language, effects like those noted by Theo Nichols commenting on what candidates write in sociology exams:

> It's a very gentle game, too. No hard knocks or shocks to received progressive opinions. Religion is "out" ("a non-empirical means to a nonempirical end"); all drugs are not equally dangerous (tobacco and alcohol are drugs too); delinquents are not evil (a matter of subculture really). If anything *were* wrong, the sociologists would tell us, and donning their social engineering hats, they would put it right.[1]

Public examination candidates, at the time of life when it matters most to know yourself, reveal for approval knowledge not worth the getting. Dreams too are not empirical in the language used at A level but we all have them, and they matter. The candidate's mother may well be hooked on socially approved amphetamines enabling her to go on living a rather thin life; his younger brother could well, like a thirteen-year-old boy from an excellently stable bourgeois family reported to me by a therapist, smoke two joints of hash to avoid recognizing the pain caused by the death of his pet hamster; the candidate is part of a subculture too—but does he know it? And so on. The subeditor gives Nichols' article the heading "Sociology as taught at A level raises a great many queries about its purpose; what good is it for these students; is it anything other than a linguistic con job?"

But surely man studies society all his life? How can we manage to make him study it so badly? By denying that personal evidence matters and denying that all should be "measured on the pulse" as Keats recommended. It is when we reveal our predilection for discussing man as some kind of machine not unlike the machines that he builds (a *taught* predilection) that we reveal the fear that can be our collective undoing as well as our individual collapse; the fear of the irrational which, since it cannot ever be entirely denied, makes us mistrustful of each other to the extent that we mistrust ourselves. We end up fearing most of all to be puzzled, to face anything that cannot quite easily be explained. And it is true that if we look through a mechanical eye genuinely human spontaneous behavior is always puzzling. It is rather like watching a bat, which has always been equated with madness in northern folklore because his jittery flight seems so purposeless and crazy. Once you have seen a bat hunting in a favorable light, in the Aegean twilight where you can just discern the insects the bat is chasing, you see what a nimble creature the bat is, how elegant and right it is.

I am not arguing a science versus art struggle here, for I am not convinced that such a division makes sound categories. Sciences are not unimaginative; arts are not unrigorous or impractical. It is a matter rather, in all human activity, of the level of involvement, of personal commitment and investment of self, that can be reached. Would this account of the personal characteristics called for in the work of a modern scientist taken from the final summary of the first three Utah conferences on the identification of creative scientific talent differ much from what you would expect of a modern artist?

It is precisely the point at which a strong and established consensus finds itself confronted with an unassimilable fact that the forces of revolution are set in motion. These forces . . . set . . . the state of knowledge in a radically new direction of development. Since the forces of revolution must be embodied in persons, what kind of person may serve as the vehicle for the change in thinking which must come? . . . The scientist must be orderly, thorough and disciplined in his acquisition of current knowledge . . . he must be prepared to stand his ground against outcries from the proponents of the previous but, in his view, no longer tenable consensus. He must possess independence of judgment and hold to his own opinion in the face of a consensus which does not fit all the facts . . . (he) must be passionately committed to his own cosmology and must respect his private intuitions, even where they seem unreasonable to himself; he must be able to open himself to sources of information which others deny themselves.[2]

All his applies of course to the creative scientist and the creative artist—two things most of us never get round to being. Are the same characteristics to be expected in some measure from all of us (bearing in mind that the description sounds like a portrait of a pretty "difficult" person)? In a settled world where there is an infrequently challenged consensus on what the world is and how it goes on, and what challenges there are rarely produce obvious innovations, it does not matter so much if people resent being uncertain. In an unsettled world everyone needs to be much more open-minded than most people now are and I have no doubt that the route to achieving the kind of personal curiosity which everyone will need to keep alive is through a restitution of the willingness to "respect private intuitions, even where they seem unreasonable." This in turn demands we interest ourselves in bases of social agreement different from the law-and-order model all governments and most teachers prefer.

Wherever areas of the social system can be opened to experiment, we must use them to explore systems of collaboration which do *not* deny that it is sense and not madness in man to have and value fantasies, intuitions and all the highly personal perceptions and oddities that make up the uniqueness of individuals and enrich us all collectively. We still have far to go to eliminate the social mechanisms which tend towards standardization of persons and to recognize that in life what feels wrong is wrong. Our generation is used to making great attempts at rather inappropriate selfcontrol by exercising a sort of procrustination on ourselves. (I derive the term from the legendary Procrustes who would trim his guests to fit the bed he offered them by lopping off any inconvenient limbs.) Many of the young are already reversing this trend by healthily asserting that if our feelings seem inconvenient because they are at odds with naive mechanical ways of organizing human behavior, we should not deny the validity of our feelings but rather question the validity of the organization and look for alternatives. This is not so much new wisdom as old wisdom resurfacing; wisdom which has been in eclipse as long as the strange doctrine of Progress has held sway, throughout the dark bleak years of industrialization in which the power blocs which still intimidate us have developed.

These recent centuries have seen a fearful rate of acceleration in the utter destruction of the natural environment of man and all awareness of the symbiotic elements in our relationship with it. Space travellers have at last succeeded in moving around in a completely man-made encapsulated environment. Our first act on the moon included dumping rubbish as well as depositing instruments and the lumber of a national flag. Much we inherit from these centuries may be gain but much is certainly loss; not only loss of environment but of human canniness. We have shifted in that time from a poor view of society as a Body Politic subject to canker to an even poorer one of a society in which man is subjected to restriction within what has come to be called "the machinery of State." We have been trained to con ourselves into behaving respectfully, even deferentially, towards much that is naturally repugnant.

Shakespeare took it for granted that men in office will be insolent. Milton forcefully reminds us that conscience, coming as he saw it from God, absolutely must not be rendered unto Caesar. I would suppose that piety too is something that belongs to God and not to Caesar—and emphatically not to Mammon. Why is it then that most of us in a "free" nation react very nervously at overt public shows of lack of respect for the authority of the State or any constituted authority? Why is half the literature of education devoted to the question of authority anyway?

I shall discuss later the effect of the common set up of schooling as a social system on this issue. It is enough to say here that the question of authority is normally one that only arises when it is put by people who have effective power over others, and that my own long experience denies that it automatically arises from the family structure. I have known many youngsters who have referred to me behavior like that offered to parents who were crushing them. When I have responded with behavior unlike that of their parents, they have had no difficulty in sharing decisions with me. I have not found either that many parents are genuinely hostile to their children's bids for freedom to grow; but I accept that this situation may be in danger of deterioration as more parents are subjected to a feeling of powerlessness within a society that becomes almost daily more patently beyond anybody's control.

It seems that a crisis must face democracy all over the world. It may well be that the simple fact of overcrowding induces a feeling of panic which diverts the aggressive drive which we are all given to build society with towards destruction rather than creation. Any talk about the constitution of human instinct is of course still highly speculative, but we should accept that instinct cannot be denied. All species have an instinctive ability to perceive dangerous situations. Even sophisticated beings like ourselves whose perceptions are very largely learned are constantly seeking danger signals. This can be seen at its simplest in London street fights between youngsters which often begin with the challenge, "You looked at me" which is recognized as justification for a "rumble." True, the code employed here is clearly understood by both parties, but random uncoded violence may have the same roots. It is likely that a good human environment is one without too many people in it and this fact, rather than worries about whether the world has enough resources, makes it a very serious matter indeed that one fifth of all the people who have ever lived are alive now. If, as I believe, the majority of us spend most of our time trying to conceal a permanent condition of panic aroused by too much contact with people we don't know, it will become less, not more, easy to control our impulses to lash out and destroy blindly.

The possession of power over others becomes more and more dangerous in these circumstances, given that the tools of power become increasingly efficient at the same time. It is not because of some notional doctrine of equality but because of a direct fear of the probable consequences that we need now to demand a halt and rapid reversal of the element in our educational system which still is intent on creating an elite and in a search for administrative talent imposes a competition for power on all our young. In Britain, despite moves towards comprehensive secondary education, most of the demands made on children stem from the elitist function of the universities. The search goes on for one particular kind of cleverness (*not* the awkward creative child who is consistently overlooked) which can be exploited. Those who possess it are rewarded for having been exploited with the right to exploit us. We destroy the potential wisdom of many of our most talented youngsters by making predators of them. These are the young who are at present under the most savage attack all over the world—the students who have understood the offer and are repudiating it, usually in terms of expressing solidarity with the workers. In the USA it has led to students being gassed and bombed; in Britain to colleges being closed, staff dismissed and students expelled; in Prague, where solidarity was achieved, to Russian invasion. It is when those who have been offered conventional power refuse it that authority is most challenged. Reform of education is made particularly difficult because what is most urgent is that teachers should repudiate the present educational system. I shall go into this more deeply later when I discuss the role of the teacher.

Those who possess authority are immediately confronted by a major problem—others have the choice of wresting it from them or of abolishing it. Teachers are inevitably caught in the crossfire. But the corner teachers find themselves in because of their profession is no tighter than the corner everybody is in—it is an acute form of a common human problem.

As Jules Henry says, there seems never to have been a time when so many people feel themselves to be shut in a room with no exit. We seem to have what we have been taught to want and yet life feels wrong: "Grazing on the grasses of affluence, the white American population is one of the most docile on earth."[3] In the docility stakes, the white populations of all the other great industrial nations, including the British, come a close second. The danger of such docility in the populations of technologically advanced states has been too well shown in the history of totalitarian states in this century to need more than a mention. But the interlock of national affairs achieved by the communication technology of the last decade and enforced by the international organization of the control of resources this technology demands increases the danger of a struggle for complete world domination. The world is suffering from a rash of nationalism which itches more insistently as personal identity becomes weaker. If we have little pride in ourselves we will seek pride in what we belong to and at a time when we most need to belong to a species, we are more violently forced to belong to nations. Try travelling without a passport. Remember that the moon now carries a national emblem.

We simply cannot afford to allow the powers our species now has to remain uncontrolled except by threat of retaliation and war between great power blocs. We cannot afford the license we have allowed ourselves in the antisocial use of our aggression; it must again become a creative tool used to guard the community and not a weapon for egocentricity in the individual or the super-individual nation-state. Alas every nation boasts most of the history of its conquests and it is in terms of the conquest of space that today's marvels are praised. It is a tall order to expect man to rid himself of the burden of such attitudes *but our survival demands it*. If we cannot rid ourselves of it soon, better we go the way of the dinosaur.

But why should we not rid ourselves of the burden? We are used to gasping at the vision of our technical powers. Why, given that, should we go on using such intellectual flint axes as intelligence tests to assess man's psychological possibilities? Given that our destruction of environment must very soon be halted and reversed into restitution wherever possible there is still nothing to fear from the way we have grown so long as we can understand ourselves and our needs as human creatures. But we have everything to fear if we cannot understand and respect our human nature.

Such an understanding does not come to us through scholastic enterprise. If it did there would not be so much nonsense psychology in print, and all the teachers who have taken courses in psychology would understand themselves and their pupils. It comes from enjoying the right kind of relationships with other human beings and from an open acknowledgment and enjoyment of our own identities. Maybe we have fled to the moon to escape having to face home truths. We are doing almost nothing to improve human relations. This is why such an attempt now urgently becomes the first task for any educational system.

It may well be that we are deliberately shielding ourselves from seeing how bad things really are because the challenge is so frightening. The scale of it is clearly expressed by Margaret Mead:

> We avoid seeing the most obvious truth of the new age: no one will live all his life in the world into which he was born and no one will die in the world in which he worked in his maturity.[4]

Such a whirlwind of changes cannot be faced by a human being brought up to depend on stability of things external to himself for a sense of satisfaction in being. For everybody, worldwide, the need is for a strong (i.e. *not* a touchily egocentric) personal identity—the resilient awkwardness characteristic of the creative scientist. Only this can ensure fulfilment of the last condition Margaret Mead imposes (my italics):

> There are far too many complaints about society having to move too fast to keep up with the machine. There are great advantages in moving fast if you move completely, if social, educational and recreational change keeps pace. You must change the whole pattern at once and the whole group together—*and the people themselves must decide to move.*[5]

Can these conditions be achieved? I think that the proposals made later in this book go further towards it than other recommended reforms of education, in that they incorporate suggestions for collaborative learning in which it is essential that the learner experiences continually learning to move together in the group. They are recommendations I think of as the *minimum* change towards meeting the demand. Clearly without efforts towards democracy elsewhere in the social system they could not be entirely effective. But the nature of the revolution we need is beyond the scope of this book. I am sure it is not one which any currently popular political language copes with.

Danilo Dolci, who may be regarded as a pioneer of the new politics we need (we cannot really call it participant democracy because this term is already used too facilely by the representative democracy parties), offers much the same assurances as Dr. Mead. He sees choosing new directions for mankind as a matter of seeking, recognizing and choosing alternatives. In this case, the individual capacity for perceiving startling possibilities becomes again highly important, but

> Valid alternatives cannot be realized without valid personalities, without new minds and a new productive capacity . . . . Society can remain fundamentally healthy only if there is a healthy interaction among its various groups and members.[6]

We shall not get these valid personalities without a continual deep concern for the *quality* of relationships, without setting up groupings in which a genuine quality can be attained, without protecting ourselves and our young from being swamped in situations of mass submersion.

Here yet again a strong cultural tradition has to be reversed. In our society we make great play with the face value of collective responsibility, but guilt we always refer to the individual. Class teaching plays a great part in establishing this particular confidence trick, helped by the fact that man is a guilt-prone creature anyway. We will not admit that collectively, as a society, we are responsible for the individual breakdowns that we are all prone to (nowadays a fifth of the population goes mentally sick at some time of life and the proportion steadily grows) nor will we yet accept that breakdown, urban violence, and war too, are all products of day to day living and working set-ups that are simply inappropriate to man. Fear of oddness becomes fear of madness (a weapon most dangerously used against adolescents) which is a fear of the retaliation of violated human nature. The more widespread this fear is, the more widespread is the urge to cling to conformity which causes the violation. We shall not find valid personalities without creating settings within which validity can grow. We must recognize the possibility of collective faults as well as collective virtue and accept responsibility for our social systems. Systems in which the simple right of human beings to relationship, to membership (*full* membership) of the species and of some protecting group within it, are not recognized; systems in which relationship is not given, but has to be earned—these must be cleared away. We are directly teaching mistrust of humanity wherever we make the young compete for esteem. There is a natural drive towards this which needs no reinforcement; indeed it needs countering and can only be countered by experience of successful collaboration with others in which everybody's selfesteem is enhanced and in which questions of esteem eventually simply fall out of mind. I find that so many people simply cannot see what I'm getting at when I talk of this "loss of self" in collective activity (which is the highest fulfilment of self and totally noncompetitive) that I must ruefully conclude that very few opportunities exist in our society to experience it. But it is visible sometimes in discotheques where teenagers dance; it is visible in improvised drama, and the best games of really fine soccer teams, where individual performance reaches its heights, yet the group is as one, no member outbidding any other. It can be seen in certain children's games which at first glance look competitive but turn out in fact to be rituals.

I am sure the feeling is recognizable to most people. But it is a devalued feeling. After all such a simple act as getting a seat on a bus in any modern city is in fact a highly competitive act; finding somewhere quiet to live is even more competitive. The pressure to opt out is so much stronger than the temptation really to give yourself by joining in, especially when there is no place physically to opt out to, and you are forced to withdraw spiritually into zombie-like apathy.

McLuhan assures us that our communication and transport technology is now sufficient to enable us to decentralize rapidly and turn the world into a tolerable global village. The alternative, as J. W. Dyckman points out, is that

> ... the population of the future city of thirty million might be compacted into dense masses. If humans living in the cities interacted like gas molecules in a closed container, or like rats in cages, increased densities could conceivably lead to overheating, or to a volume of contact which would overload the individual's capacity for response and result in behaviour breakdown. Studies on lower animals, such as rats, suggest that this outcome is a serious possibility. However there are a number of reasons for believing that this outcome cannot be extended to humans by simple analogy ... humans have a capacity for creating internal order behind the protective wall of privacy .... It must be recognized however that the

personal defences which secure this internal order may at times become pathological and lead to social disorder. Privacy may be secured by depersonalization, or by withdrawing entirely into oneself. While the anomie observed by nineteenth century sociologists is one pathological form, a kind of involuntary privacy, the selfconcern of bystanders who watch murder and mayhem in a subway without intervening, is another form.[7]

This is the danger of the city (and of the classroom and of any standardizing mass situation), that to defend ourselves we must become our own enemy by dwindling to something less than human. The architect Doxiadis puts the case very simply:

> I feel that I am in danger but this is not the first time it has happened either to me or to my city. The day before yesterday Athens was burned by the Persians; yesterday Athenians were dying in the streets because of the starvation imposed by the occupation forces of the Axis. We are always endangered by something but in this case there is one difference: the danger is continuous and in all centres of civilization—if it continues there is nothing that can save us. In this respect it is a unique danger for humanity. The present city, without reason, without dream, leads to dystopia and disaster.[8]

All the centres of civilization (which used not to be the dirty word it must now surely become) are knit together. I have not stood by and watched a murder in a New York street but I have sat in front of my television set and watched a Vietnamese child burned to a frazzle in a jelly of blazing napalm without intervening, without seriously believing I could force the government which "represents" me to intervene. And so probably, have you.

Dennis Enright puts the more complicated case even more simply:

Times have changed.
Remember the helplessness
Of the serfs,
The inexplicable Tyrannies
Of the lords.

But times have changed.
Everything is explained to us
In expert detail.
We trail the logic of our lords
Inch by inch.

The serfs devised religions
And sad and helpful songs.
Sometimes they ran away.
There was somewhere to run to.
Times have changed.[9]

This takes us to the heart of the matter. Our defenselessness because of our habitual modes of withdrawal is deepened by the erosion of language (which Marcuse in *One Dimensional Man* takes two chapters to trace) which goes with mass media and can only be countered by the leisurely experience of talking to people about things which matter. This needs urgently to be restored in education. Machine programmed instruction enables our lords to expose their logic to us millimetre by millimetre, and useful as programming may be as a clear exposition of noncontroversial information, spending more time at it means spending even less time in dialogue with people. You *can* fool all of the people all of the time if you coarsen language enough by academic exercises in one-way "communication" and by limiting its more tentative, exploratory uses at times when through extended skirmishing we come to share our meanings. Our language is as Dr. Leavis has rightly said, "the greatest collaborative achievement of man" and talking is collaborating in a search for significance.

I am not suggesting a life of Socratic dialogue, nor that the early years of life should be spent crosslegged under the banyan tree, but that the *silence* of schools should go, and the demand be fulfilled which is made by the fourteen-year-old Sicilian girl Bruna, whose critique of her schooling is reported by Dolci:

> I'll tell you what it's really like: we mustn't do anything to harm one another, we must respect our elders and betters and so on—but we can't have opinions. There's no question of me having my say, and then you having your say, and then discussing the thing till we reach some conclusion that suits us all. We mustn't do anything to *harm* one another—but there's no question of me actually *helping* you, or you helping me.

What is needed is to protect the right to act in situations where dialogue is possible, and where it is expected that people will have opinions about what they're doing and much else besides. Bernstein has shown how the rejection of infants' opinions and questions in many proletarian homes encapsulates them in a restricted code which excludes them from playing any part in the different language offered them in schools. But in most schools another equally severely restricted code is in use—again a language code bonded to a behavioral code appropriate to a rigid social system, as Douglas Barnes shows in a very effective, cool study of classroom language.[11] And there are other restricted codes too, such as that of advertising, which invites you to become involved through your recognition that the statements being made are not literal, and the Newspeak of politics.

We should have no doubt that the issue is most serious. We hint all the time to the young that there is something indecent even in questioning the definitions of the world and of ourselves we are offered. As Stokely Carmichael says: "The ones who make the definitions are the masters." It follows that all of us who simply accept definitions and feel uneasy when they are challenged are slaves. Many of the masters are slaves too; only a grand master is not restricted by his own definitions. But we become reliant on definitions only when we are restricted from much talking and have no experience of the tentativeness of language. It is restricting people to silent social systems where opinions wilt because of familiarity with blunt rejection or the acid of ridicule which causes the erosion of public language and the consequent concealment of the realities we face. Who is faring well in the Welfare State? R. D. Laing puts the dangers very pungently:

> Many people are tortured by contradictions that exist only between facts and propaganda, not in the facts themselves. For instance we have *not* abolished poverty within our own territory. The USA is *not* a democracy. Once you think the USA is not a democracy, then there are a great many problems that do not have to be resolved, because they do not exist . . . . We do not have to ask why an increasing number of the world's inhabitants hate us Europeans and the USA. We do not have to go into extraordinary psychological explanations of why I would hate somebody who had napalmed my children.[1][2]

The time really has come for a reappraisal of our investment policies of human energies. We must stop looking upon the social scene, saying it is good and resting from our labors. We should be breaking down the old consensus as it has broken down in the natural sciences and be seeking a new one. Our first reaction is always to justify ourselves, but what do we find if we measure the gap between our human powers and our social achievements?

We can invent materials of such extraordinary properties that we can shelter from any environment, however hostile. We can travel and forage and sustain life in the depths of the oceans, the deepest bowels of the earth, in the atmosphere which surrounds us, and way out in the mathematical buzzing beyond that, where unthinkably vast treasures of energy lie. In the whole of human history until now we had only scratched at our earth's skin and dredged the shallows of the seas. In the lifetime of children still in our primary schools we have broken those bounds with a wild inventiveness.

But look at the obsolete and squalid rubbish we are building today on the earth—new cities worse than the old which have been thrown up with less concern than mankind has ever shown for the realities of human biology.

We are within biting distance of actually making forms of life from inert matter. Spare-part surgery is such a commonplace that it would not be surprising to come across a poster today proclaiming a national transplant week. We have birth control and death control.

But nobody in his right mind would call us healthy. We have a longer life of well regulated diseases, most of them caused simply by living as unnaturally as we do.

We have extended our brains by inventing computers, data storage and information transfer systems so complex and rapid that they already are becoming super persons, putting very great power in a few hands. When they all get together there really will be nowhere to hide and no human recordable attribute will be able to remain hidden, though there may be much of our humanity yet to lose. The positive gain is an enormous increase in our power to evaluate fact and to check up on the validity of hypotheses.

But we still bury ourselves and our young under tons of dead information as if we still needed to memorize and allow outmoded opinions to masquerade as facts. We cannot really get to know our neighbors because we have all been made so wary of intimacy by being misunderstood, misinterpreted, labelled, and stigmatized by the labels people have stuck on us that we have learned that anonymity is the better part of identity.

And the realities are sicker than the sickest joke any of us could invent. If my suggestion of a national transplant week seems ludicrous—well, didn't the hysterical press acclamation of the first heart transplant just about amount to that? And what about this perfectly serious newspaper report:

> The Anatomical Donations and Post Mortem Examinations Bill before Parliament this week gives the Minister of Health total control over transplants of male or female reproductive organs if the purpose of the transplants is to assist procreation . . . . The committee was told that although a successful gonad transplant resulting in actual procreation had not been performed anywhere yet 'it is not impossible that it will be performed in the future.' (Some authorities think a gonad transplant would not be as difficult as a kidney transplant.)
>   Gonad transplants would throw up the whole question of recipients of one colour receiving reproductive organs from donors of another colour.[1][3]

This is not a state of affairs worth justifying. Fortunately it will not be possible to go on justifying it much longer unless censorship is universally imposed on all media. The gap between technological and social growth is too obvious. Most of the world's population is young and accustomed to rapid change from birth. Indeed childhood itself shortens for each generation. And the worldwide effect of film, radio and television is to show the wealthy and the powerful to the poor and the powerless. The inegalities of affluence and of human rights will not be accepted with the old patience. The revolution this time has preceded the political organization; the worst of the troubles are yet to come.

The alternatives are clear; either a revolution in education—a shared move into the future by all generations working out a new society together designed to transcend nationalism—or disaster, conflict on a scale never seen yet. We must learn to collaborate better, to eradicate divisions which, whatever purposes they may have served in the past, can now serve for no good ends or we risk the extinction of the whole human species, since weapons which could destroy us all will be in many hands and their spread cannot be contained by agreements made between the present dominant super states.

All this perhaps goes some way to answering my original

questions. But even the more short-sighted answers which are possible if we look only at our own internal national condition tend to the same conclusions. The dangers facing affluent industrial man, the difficulty of ensuring his continued possession of all that we mean by humanity, are in some ways made more acute by the ways in which our affluence is most likely to increase, i.e. by a shift towards automation and the revolution in working life which that will bring about.

The future that many people predict and give two faint cheers for is one in which work disappears or becomes a privilege reserved for a brilliant few. There are grounds for believing that this would be a disaster for most men, and if women are not to be allowed to breed they too are at risk of losing the role for which all our traditions prepare them. We do not know what chance there is of ritualistic activities "taking up the slack" of workless lives. Rituals are after all meant to be productive in primitive societies and if we are to think of them as merely symbolic, there seems little ground for indulging in them. What is left for the workless would seem to be the old aristocratic occupations of politics, hunting, or patronage of the arts. Politics, of the old kind, is out. So is hunting in an overpopulated world. Pursuit of the arts demands an under-standing of them which is only acquired by devotion and a willingness to enter into the struggle with that uncertainty which is at the root of all creation. This again would mean that a high personal tolerance of ambiguity at present found in a small minority would become necessary for everybody. Bread and circus shows and petty hobbies satisfy only people who are tired and fretful from rather tedious work.

But this prediction may well be wrong. It is already possible for a designer alone with his machinery to set up a production line for custom-built goods and we can certainly expect this to spread to all production. But computers do far more than exclude people both from directly productive work and from distribution of goods (which can just as readily be automated as production can). They also eat up and breed information, and give rise to a quite new information technology in which many scanners are needed to support fewer programmers. For example in the USA it is forecast that there will be at least one million more jobs for programmers in the next ten years and this is a trade still in its infancy. The future then is for artists, inventors and people highly expert in some field of information—all trades demanding the characteristics of small minorities in the past.

It is at least arguable that schooling as we have hitherto imposed it has destroyed far more talent than it has ever fostered because it has not sought to foster individual talent at all, only to encourage such few as were needed for particularly prestigious trades and with a preference for docile candidates even for them. Where we cannot predict exactly the behavior trades will demand (and we no longer can) the old procedures of sifting and grading become irrelevant. They are so inbuilt into almost everything we do in schools now that they will be very hard to throw off. But thrown off they must be. The very worst way to help people to become more resilient is to nail them down to safe routines. And we ourselves who deal with the young must grow, if not to welcome uncertainty, at least not to fear it.

If we cannot bring ourselves to prefer the tentative to the definitive, to mistrust the routines with which we have defended ourselves from awareness of the pace of change, we will inevitably go on trying to break the spirit of anyone in whom we see such a mistrust developing, killing off the only kind of questing spirit that can save us all from further dehumanization. The viability of personality that Dolci calls for is inborn; it is destroyed by the kinds of restraint we put on our curiosity, our primate heritage. Every time any question is deemed improper or closed, the vision of man's possibilites shrinks again.

But it is just this personal picture of our own opportunities and of the opportunities of man as a species that makes up the identity we shall need—or rather we need now, in a world which never stands still.

Summary

I have reviewed the scope of enquiry needed to make decisions on educational policy and concluded:

1. Change is too rapid to allow any prediction to be valid except the prediction that even more change will come even more rapidly.
2. Further attempts to stabilize society at present are likely to destroy democracy utterly.
3. The only defense is to help people acquire a new kind of valid personality which is nonhostile to others, noncompetitive, and assured of a personal capacity to discover order.
4. This personality is of the kind hitherto identified as creative and tends to be awkward and resist authority.
5. We need to transcend both personal egocentricity and the displaced egocentricity of competitive nationalism.
6. A new awareness of our nature as a species will be needed and is needed already.
7. We must re-examine the social systems which block the development of valid personality. This includes our educational systems.
8. All this holds good even for our future national economic advantage.

References

1. Theo Nichols, "The Sociology Game," in *New Society* (July 31, 1969).
2. Calvin Taylor and Frank Warren, *Scientific Creativity* (John Wiley, 1963).
3. Jules Henry, "Social and Psychological Preparations for War," in *The Dialectics of Liberation*, David Cooper, ed. (Penguin, 1968).
4. Margaret Mead, in *Time* (September 4, 1954).
5. See note 4 above.
6. Danilo Dolci, *For the Young* (MacGibbon and Kee, 1967).

7. John W. Dyckman, "Some Conditions of Civic Order in an Urbanized World," in *Daedalus* (summer 1966).
8. Constantin Doxiadis, *Between Dystopia and Utopia* (Faber, 1968).
9. D. J. Enright, *The Old Adam* (Hogarth Press, 1965; Wesleyan University Press, 1965).
10. See note 6 above.
11. D. R. Barnes, "Language in the Secondary Classroom," in *Language, the Learner and the School* (Penguin, 1969).
12. R. D. Laing, "The Obvious," in *The Dialectics of Liberation*, David Cooper, ed. (Penguin, 1968).
13. *Johannesburg Sunday Times* (June 22, 1969).

CHAPTER 2

Changes in Adolescence

So far I have discussed the common human problems, the needs we all have, which an educational system should be designed to meet. Since we are not starting from scratch (it would be easier if we could) but are faced instead with the problem of changing an unsatisfactory system into a more satisfactory one, I have at this stage to accept some limits. I will allow myself a much more speculative chapter at the end of this book, but here I must accept that the situation we are faced with is one in which the main tool of education is what goes on when teachers and youngsters meet in schools. It is secondary schools I am concerned with, places where adults meet adolescents.

If we take it that the common problems belong to us all, whatever our age, we still have to consider whether there are problems which are peculiar to adolescents and whether a knowledge of these should further influence our policy decisions.

As with all knowledge, our knowledge of adolescence depends on the questions we are prepared to put and I think there is very little we do know about it as a process. So many pressures are brought to bear on youngsters of this age, so much role learning has already gone on, that it is difficult to know whether we are describing the creature or its environment.

If Freud is right, what we are witnessing in adolescents is a revivification of conflicts suppressed since infancy. The deepest defeat we ever suffer is not at the hands of our parents but at the infantile recognition of our impotence; aware of our sexual need, we are aware of our inability to fulfil it. We cannot possess or rival our parents fully so we retreat into childhood, reassuring ourselves of our parents' love and shelter if we are lucky enough to have convincing evidence of either; many unfortunates do not find this reassurance. Puberty, signalling the growth which will give us the power to rival adults and fulfil sexual desire, opens the old conflicts abruptly. Internally the event is most disturbing. We have learned ways of coping which will no longer do. We are *very* expert children; but childhood is a defense with its own strategies and they are no longer appropriate.

It is interesting and inexplicable that childhood is becoming much shorter; the young spend much less of their lives in this defensive phase. What difference this makes to our whole pattern of learning I cannot say, but the whole balance of life is certainly altered radically where childhood shrinks and adolescence stretches out as it now does into our mid-twenties. It ends only when we are accepted fully as adults, which in our society means doing a job on equal terms with people of any age, not just having achieved a mating.

Our youngsters are contained in our secondary schools throughout the years of early and mid-adolescence, coping first with the surprise of sexual potency and rapid growth, and then with discovering and building into a new, reorganized identity the new elements of power. Everyone suffers some shock and uncertainty in the process; it is a period of experimental identity. In the old world one expected this to be concluded by maturity. I doubt the possibility of such a conclusion any more and expect adolescence to provide skill in experiment rather than a final answer, since our lifelong need will be to go on finding new answers to new, identity disturbing questions.

If a boy begins playing Hamlet when he has been cast as Guildenstern or Othello, a quarrel arises on stage which can only be resolved by referring to the producer. As school teachers we like to claim the powers of Pygmalion wherever we think our students succeed and blame the parents wherever the result is not so good; we are tempted to play the part of the producer.

But the teacher is not the producer. He is simply one of the characters in the drama being played out in the school, a drama for which there is no script and no producer. There are guidelines—patterns of expectation, a linguistic style, and assumptions about roles—but within that framework all is improvisation. Even so the role of learner *offered* the adolescent in school is more clearly marked out than the role of adolescents as a group in society.

Members of stable societies (and yesterday's, however volatile it seemed was more stable than today's) have roles of an appropriate kind assigned to them at all ages, expressed in detailed assumptions which could emerge in expressions such as calling a woman "mutton dressed as lamb" and in a very clear code of deferences. The curriculum of our schools is always a tidier and somewhat old-fashioned version of a system of values we are trying to induce the young to share, calculated on the forecasts of the state of the labor market they will be entering. At present it seems to reflect the assumption that adolescence is a time of life when all is waiting, and nothing doing. Should we reverse this and try to demonstrate that a great deal is doing, indicate the possibilities and help the young to achieve the possibilities they choose for themselves? Once we could pretend there was a time of life for mastering information followed by years of using that information unrevised. That is certainly not true now.

Where roles are poorly defined we have to improvise and improvisation itself may become a way of life—and a good one at that. A fixed role is replaced by a greater flexibility of personal responses by all people involved, across and within generations. The notion that people have *given* roles to play in our society, and *given* ways to play them, that there is a script to be learned and repeated, is of course bureaucratically attractive. It is easier to set up and very easy to control. But it is leading us to offer the young an invitation to exhaust and debilitate themselves by going uphill with the brakes on. Life is already for all of us a matter of identifying the challenges which face us *now*, expecting them *not* to be familiar, *not* to be settled by routine. Could we not then share the experience with our young and put at the centre of our concern for them a hope to help them deal with the problems they see as personally immediate? In this case we must get to know them well and enable them to know us, well enough for us jointly to identify the inhibitory processes that may be hampering them.

This is a crucial point. How well we know each other depends on the social system within which we meet. If a new curriculum is to be evolved from a better knowledge of needs, it is not to be achieved without a new way of running schools. No amount of tinkering with information and repackaging it and keeping it up to date will do. The answers to the vital question "What help do young people need to get from teachers and what help can teachers give them?" lies in the further question "In what conditions can help be given?"

The question is not to be answered hastily. Adolescents do not readily verbalize the needs with which they are, after all, experimenting. We must make some guesses of our own and explore the teacher/pupil relationship in some detail.

When he labelled societies which function by a division of labor "anomic" (without norms) Durkheim put his finger on a sore point that has become more troublesome as our society's industrialism has become more sophisticated. Societies survive only by virtue of the agreements made within them and agreements are more easily reached the more readily people see that they have common ground. This is as true of nations as it is of individuals or of subcultures. To pass on a system of values so fixed that there is never any question of what you do to be doing the right thing, of the appropriate behavior, is impossible in an anomic society. With no real backing from tradition to support them in their dealings with the young, most adults will nevertheless feel tempted to preach a security they are unlikely to feel very deeply themselves. If as I have suggested childhood is mainly defensive, children will be predisposed to accept and at times even to demand such pretenses. This process can go wrong even more easily than the withdrawal defense we put up to protect ourselves from overexposure to contact in city life.

All too often adults are not rid of their own childhood. Resentful of the speed of change around them, they may be seeking external support for an inadequate identity. The more they feel threatened by their own freedom, the less freedom they will offer to their young; or rather the less assurance that freedom is to be enjoyed rather than feared. The freedom they do allow will be hedged about with reassurances which indicate that freedom is fearful. Obvious lack of confidence in our children is as damaging to them as downright hostility.

Many of us seem to be all at sea when it comes to deciding about even trivial issues of personal freedom. We are still living with the fairy tale belief (part of the fairy tale about the perfectibility of civilization) that if humanity let its hair down it would become savage. This is as nonsensical as any hope of attaining savagery via drugs, rock, and ritual without completely reconstituting savage social organization and religious perception. Savagery is a sophisticated way of life. It is the brutality of civilized urban man that is easy to achieve.

Savage societies have a stability to offer—patterns of highly ritualized appropriate behavior and belief. They build no cities; they keep their communities small and inviolate. Unlike our villagers they pay no tribute to cities. They sense and make legends of a symbiotic relationship both with other creatures and with spirits. Their identity, though rich, is soft edged and their sense of continuity of the community is so strong that every birth is more a rebirth of a known spirit than the arrival of a stranger. There is mythical support for the way of life, but the essence of the way of life is the stability of the small community within which people can genuinely know each other. The certainties which the individual gets from this are most unlike the iron code of "thou shalts" and "thou shalt nots" which institutional urban man sees as unfreedom but often hankers after. The benefit for the savage is what Lévi-Strauss calls "authenticity of knowledge." Of our own way of life he comments:

> Of course even in western societies there are levels of authenticity in the form of institutional or noninstitutional groups in which individual members have concrete

knowledge of each other. But nonauthentic levels are on the increase: I mean all those ways in which actual people are cut off from each other or interconnected only through intermediary agents or a system of relays, such as administrative machinery or ideological ramifications.

We need

... decentralization in all fields, so that the greatest number of social and economic activities could be carried out on the level of authenticity at which the members of a given group have a concrete knowledge of each other.[1]

Authenticity of this kind may in fact produce great flexibility; it certainly does not produce the urge to standardize individuals. The norms of such a society are complex in practice.

But in our anomic society we attempt to govern behavior by reference to what is normal, while at the same time we accept that we cannot offer norms which are universally appropriate. Notions of propriety become a matter of awareness of "what is done" in specific group situations; the only behaviors universally excluded (on the face value system) are those which are held to be appropriate to a defined criminal subculture. Meanwhile the face value system itself readily accepts "Thou shalt not kill—unless in uniform."

We have no teachable certainties. They were the price we paid for our numbers, our economic organization and our mobility. If we are to have no certainties we have to accept that all values are called into question and are to be questioned at all times and that this applies to the values of all groups equally. All will be changeable, if not volatile. It is this which has prevented education becoming purely a "bourgeoisification" process of the whole population in those capitalist States where popular expectations and the dominance of bourgeois values seem to indicate that this is what schooling is for.

Here we are confronted with the dilemma which must afflict a society with face values founded on human rights applied to the individual and working values which rely on nonauthentic

59

contacts. A mass society can drift along in this way only so long as actual direct conflicts can be coped with at a newspaper headline level and described as isolated peculiar incidents. But in fact it is crazy to think that without clearly marked territorial boundaries, with rapidly increasing population making all personal stresses more acute, the conflicting values of groups can just rub shoulders and pass each other by. The source of values lies in small groups, not in the individual. An individual on his own can cause very little trouble without allies. Standardization, the tool of the old educational system, makes or confirms alliances by teaching us officially that we have these or those limits because we are deprived, or born stupid, or deaf, or black. Know thy stigmata and so know thyself. It is all very well to argue as Ian Taylor does that "Ideally, we simply ought to learn to live with soccer hooliganism without panicking. It is a result of rearguard activities by the weak and poorly placed."[2] But this involves inviting somebody to accept the risk of being set upon and kicked raw in the street if he happens to be in the area of a football stadium within an hour of the end of a sensitive match; it is not just an appeal to a great public not to be overly shocked by news of another incident. The advice is even less helpful to any citizen of Chicago or to an Ibo Nigerian or a Hausa Nigerian. Values are not like streams of water of different temperatures which have only to meet to find a new common level. Our attachment to our values (the small group values, not the publicized face values of our notional society) is deep enough to constitute much of our identity.

So it is not enough to argue a historical justification for the doubly threatening conflicts in which young people will find themselves involved, doubly threatening because they not only become entangled with unconscious conflicts with their parents, but also because they demand even more questioning of an identity already shaken by growth. We can have a society only when all the groups to which we belong, and which belong to us in that we play an effective part and are not merely accepted in them, productively collaborate. This is why it will not be sufficient for our young just to learn to have better personal relationships. The lesson to be learned from any improvement of personal relationship is that the improvement comes when we manage not to hide our conflicts, but bring them out into the light and resolve them. We do not merely learn to live with them.

For instance the femininity, the *difference* of women, is a threat to impotent men and to little boys. It frightens men to be aware of any dependence on creatures so unlike themselves. The fear is not admitted but to repudiate it most men in our civilization are led at some stage of their development to repudiate femininity as if it could intrude into them and weaken their maleness. A phoney "butch" maleness is the product which itself produces conflict with the women they approach. A tiny drop-out minority evades the conflict altogether by never approaching women and some even seek to take over a feminine personality and pay high surgical fees to have the body trimmed—a case of "Snip, snip, and Bob's your aunty."[3] But it is not the difference between men and women which causes this conflict and most of us lose the fear of the other sex when we find what pleasure it can give us.

I have taken this fundamental business of personal relationships here to outline the process which operates in all our relationships. As we come to discover more of the uniqueness of other people we discover that differences enhance us and diversity enriches us—this is what allows conflicts to be resolved. We learn to live with conflicts only where we turn our backs on each other, letting underlying fears keep the upper hand. In marriages which do not end in divorce such a situation leads to the home becoming a battlefield on which our children learn to be fearful and wary of love. Divorce would be a better resolution.

But groups within a society cannot divorce each other as couples can nor can they effectively ignore each other. They used to. There used to be somewhere to go to in a world where significant differences of local environment still existed, where communications were poor, where there were empty areas to take over, or uncrowded places where new arrivals had at least an initial welcome, and nation did not have to speak unto nation, or at least not often. None of this is now possible. The panic being shown most clearly by all the right wing politicians of the world (the putting down of the Black Panthers in the USA; the new immigration control laws in Britain; the steady extension of police powers and blatant xenophobia; the renewed attack on the freedom of writers in Russia) is a panic of groups being forced to notice each other, to admit a level of interdependence that is unfamiliar and frightening. And this panic is referred not only to the confronting groups. It is referred right back to the individual. It may very well be that the troubles of anomic society were already much more acute than anybody thought when they were first identified and that even then they were only relieved by the massive emigrations then in vogue. They can certainly not be resolved now by the old means—neither by tolerance, which only works if flight is an open final possibility, nor by referring the problem to the individual as one for his solitary selfmanipulation. There comes a limit to man's ability to adapt. While I am sure, with Dolci, that the answer lies in the validity of personality, I am equally aware that personality is a social product. The answer I am proposing may be too weak and too late but the essence of it is that for schools at least we have to establish the viability of a new social system in which we do not overload the individual with contact, do not exploit individual guilt, and do seek both the enjoyment of small value-generating groups and effective collaboration of groups.

I shall explore fully later how this would disturb even the minutiae of our current behavior in schools. Here I would only stress that we must not go on underestimating the size of the challenge individualism presents to the individual as well as to the community. In a time when philosophy (and perhaps especially the philosophy of education) seems to be seeking to become the apotheosis of anomie, it will not do for us all to become more philosophical, for it is a heavy burden to have to make our own decisions all the time and we will end up, like the professionals, only tackling the problems which don't much matter, leaving the heart issues either to chance or to authority which comes to the same thing—a fate to be accepted philosophically. The demand (and the risk of withdrawal from it) becomes excruciatingly acute when, in adolescence, we are nagged into making decisions we have no clearly acknowledged right to carry out. (The choice whether or not to obey is no genuine exercise in making decisions; we can only decide confidently if we have no uncertainty about our right to decide.) Where face values conflict with working values identity is disrupted. Fearful individualism is as disruptive of the individual as it is of society. Only when we know that we can reach working agreements with other people about both immediate and long-term common purposes can we flourish as individuals. The acquisition of this confidence becomes the major social task of all members of a democratic industrial society; there is no other way to self-fulfillment.

Here in particular most of our schools are failing us. It seems that the relationship between teachers (as a group always and as individuals mostly) and their adolescent charges still conforms to the model appropriate to hierarchic static societies and not to the freestyle mobile life of yesterday nor to the new mobility of today. Yesterday's mobility was a matter of shifting your ground; today's is more like that of the actor running on the spot who achieves his mobility by the speed of his reactions to the environment shown on the scenery whirling past him on rollers. The double charge against our schools is that we seem not only to be desperately trying to nail the scenery down, but that our efforts are directed not towards inviting students into a working partnership to learn the ways of the world but in persuading them to do as we want without feeling resentful, or without offering any evidence of such resentment as they may feel. When the system which enables us to do this is described by a clear eyed hostile observer like Jonathan Kozol,[4] we are likely to be shocked that such schools as he describes still exist. But the Boston schools he describes are *as systems* indistinguishable from our own and though we may not be working directly to achieve the aims set out in the Boston Schools Board's *Curriculum Guide in Character Education* we behave just as we would if those were our aims. They read like a caricature of a Victorian parson:

> Character traits to be developed: obedience to duly
> constituted authority ... selfcontrol ... responsibility ...
> gratitude ... kindness ... good workmanship and per-
> serverance ... loyalty ... teamwork ... honesty ... fair
> play.[5]

An identikit picture of a robot? But isn't this list very like our order of priorities inside the school?

This system not only cannot achieve the fashionable aim of "training the young in making personal decisions" (an aim I find both insufficient and unrealistic), it also reduces social life to the level of teamwork which foils any genuine attempt at collaboration. If the young are to become decision-making adults they need to be decision-making youngsters sharing the definition of the problems to be resolved. No sharing, no decision-making. Confident behavior is only to be achieved by long, successful rehearsals. The young need extensive, internalized, fully grasped concepts of self, of society and of agreements if they are to think before they act. But these concepts simply cannot be derived from precept; face value versions of them may be verbalized but they cannot become working values unless they have in fact worked. They can grow only in situations where young people are not inhibited from showing openly what they feel to be their real selves and can learn that their real selves can achieve, without throttling the springs of life, real selfsatisfaction through reaching agreements.

It is on our willingness to redesign schools as social systems, to change radically our view of how we will relate to young people as groups and to each other as members of groups of teachers that progress in education now depends, rather than on our approach to "subjects"—though that indeed matters too. But it is our values that determine what we will be concerned to learn and values are not given and not passed on; they are generated. Working values are generated in small groups where people have authentic knowledge of each other. This holds good whether traditions are strong or weak, whether the values generated are like or unlike those of preceding generations. People are left valueless not when a collapse of traditional values happens (face values get so out of phase with working values that many people overtly reject them) but when contact is too impoverished for authenticity to be achieved and for new values to be generated.

A school can either gear itself to generating values or it can reinforce the social anomie and personal alienation of youngsters and teachers alike by ordering itself on the bureaucratic model of all State enterprises and making a continuous unresolved conflict of the clashes between values brought in by youngsters and teachers. However inappropriate this system may be to life as it goes on all around outside, it becomes a totem for the teachers, one they have a strong vested interest in defending, and they will come to make their own mythology of society to support their inaccurate reading of social structures. Thus we find a tendency for teachers to believe rather readily (along with many other social speculations) that our society is witnessing the "break up of the family" which is of itself damaging and jump to the dubious conclusion that teachers now have to give the values children used to get from the family, just as we give children talking practice if they come from restricted code homes.

It is not the modern permissive and loving parental role that they arrogate to themselves but that of an authoritarian father; and teachers are doing this at a time when many parents are for very good reasons shedding precisely that role in favor of others that work better. The dangers arising from overinvestment of feeling within the small family because most other contacts in the world are inauthentic are not new. Victorian literature is rich in confessions of damage caused by parents who ran the tribal home with a rod of iron and none of the generosity a monkey leader shows. These of course were the bourgeois families of the kind whose passing causes most expressions of regret. There is far more to regret in the passing of the working class extended family and there is certainly a need in our society for more opportunities for authentic relationships *outside* the parent and children group. But where the family is not selfenclosing, relationships in small families can be better than those found in larger families, in that children and parents together share more decisions. Parents who really have trouble with their adolescents had trouble with them in infancy too. In very many families these troubles do not arise; there is room and time enough for agreements to be reached and less arbitrary law making.

But children who have more emotional elbow room at home will ask for it from teachers too. They will not get on with teachers who cannot be questioned as their parents can. Teachers who adopt an authoritarian parent type role, clinging for their own protection in a highly stressful situation to a picture of the kind of order the world no longer needs, demonstrate by their easily discerned attitudes, by the limits they set to authentic contact, a belief (which may be entirely contradictory to all they say) that all change is change for the worse and that all growth is dangerous. They prefer the youngsters to go on playing the defensive and dependent role of expert children.

The family in our society is far from breaking up; it is changing and it could change more for the better. It is not surprising that young people, while still having a need for their teachers which is *not* a need for parent substitutes, express more confidence in the support they get from their parents than in the help they get from their teachers in learning to be adult. Parents do not if they are wise just offer their children an untrammelled right to decide for themselves, but they do give a right to share fairly in any decisions that have to be made. At the crisis of the youngsters' inevitable breakaway there is likely to be a deterioration of the relationship and some fairly bitter rows, but they are the kind of rows people have who care about each other and usually the relationships recover on a new basis of equality after a fairly short time.

At home youngsters share in making decisions; in school they are subjects of an authority which usually when challenged turns out to be arbitrary. This authority masquerades as a parental kind of concern but turns out to care very little for anything but its own selfperpetuation.

Teachers need to catch up with the subtle shift of relationships within families produced by a widespread shift fom a large

66

to a small family pattern, which has led to a greater than traditional readiness to share argument and decisions. All changes demand other changes which will either seize and make the most of new opportunities or compensate for genuine losses in human experience.

If there is any truth in the assertion that families are breaking up it lies in two areas of family life where discontinuity appears to occur. Firstly, the young leave their families earlier and so the parents are younger when their children leave home; secondly a young couple on marrying are more likely to live at a distance from their own parents and siblings, so that their children are brought up with much less intimate contact with grandparents, aunts, uncles and cousins. While this is happening within the family, a similar dispersal is taking place within the community, despite greater population density. There is less intimate neighborliness, less continuity in jobs which are central to community life; the milkman changes often; the shopkeeper is not a rooted familiar person—the supermarket is killing the corner sweetshop anyway; police officers ride about in cars. There are few stable knowable people around. Mobility and economic rationalization are influencing all trades and the childhood folklore of adult life has lost its steady roots.

This lack of stable figures who may be known intimately and long enough for youngsters' understanding of them to develop and change over the years, truncates both in depth and in extent the experience of adults they need to compose a repertoire of examples of genuine adult behavior. We have to know people quite well to identify ourselves with them or to rehearse what we intend to be, and youngsters need to know numbers of adults well if they are to rehearse all the possibilities that strike them in the years of fluctuating selfhood that characterize mid-adolescence especially. Sensitive literature can be a help if it is read bearing in mind what is already known of people and helps to deepen this knowledge. It cannot help if adolescents have no real experience against which to measure the literature. Most of the "real" people encountered via the mass media have been trimmed for show and are exercises in publicity rather than selves.

The needs of adolescence have not changed. But there is great pressure for some of them to become more urgent earlier and there are also those I have talked of above which are unfulfilled by normal modern social conditions. This gives me two groups of concerns which need to be more directly provided for in our schooling.

The first group of concerns centres on the fact that although young people reach full adult status earlier and the mating urge is correspondingly more urgent earlier, their education is prolonged. They naturally heatedly resent anything that looks to them like an attempt to deny them their rights. Our picture of adolescent delinquency is largely composed of covert status quarrels. We don't allow the young legitimately to drive and own cars although they still hunger to do so, and so one of the most popular crimes of young men is "taking and driving away." A great deal of delinquency needs to be redefined as growth, or at least we need to look for different modes of resolving status struggles and clarify our reasons for insisting on keeping certain kinds of activities only for ourselves. This goes as much for sexual liaison as for anything else. We are still prone to discuss wholehearted love affairs in terms of premarital intercourse. Becoming more permissive, we act as if the experience of love should be a rehearsal of marriage, which is excusable on those grounds but not for its own sake. The result of this is to hasten marriages, despite the fact that for many, who remain students and are not economically independent, marriage is not likely to be purchasable until some ten or fifteen years after sexual maturity. If for those others who begin full time work as soon as possible marriage becomes economically viable at seventeen or eighteen, they need to be preparing for it while they are still at school. The acquisition of the complex appropriate attitudes and wide range of relevant human experience of intimate relationship can't be hustled through in a year. The *quality* of social experience the young have makes or breaks their marriages. They need to have lived personally, to be used to perceiving people as human in their fullness and their oddness, and to have been perceived themselves as such. If they are to breed (and this is certainly the driving wish of girls who marry young) they will also need to have had some acquaintance with babies and to have direct knowledge of human growth. Boys as well as girls need to *enjoy* relationship with human infants at the time of life when we are more likely to be teaching them biology by giving them dead frogs to dissect. In the typical modern family which is small with no great age spread, they may never have had a chance to handle babies and the girl who has never done this is at a severe disadvantage when it comes to nursing her own first born and may suffer needless anxieties which can vitiate her relationship with her child.

The style of education called for by such needs as these is obvious. Nobody can tell you what holding, cleaning and cuddling a baby is all about, nor can anybody tell you what loving is. Loving and caring are only to be learned by years of living in a community of people who love and care and do so overtly.

Even then a change both of style and curriculum to cope with such preparation for marriage does not cope with those who need sexual expression without marriage; and it certainly does not cope with the problem we have to face as a species of achieving sexual expression and fulfillment without breeding. Just to stabilize the world population at the present level of births per couple is going to lead to unbearable overcrowding. The warnings of those who believe we must immediately reduce birthrate below the western norm must be taken seriously and marriage may not be an appropriate model of relationship for the future at all. Since it is the last licensed area for spontaneity this is a deeply serious issue, for if spontaneity is displaced from that relationship it must be discovered in other areas where it is now frowned on.

The second group of considerations also centre on new vicissitudes of an adolescent need as old as humanity but made more acute as it gets harder to know adults other than our parents. The stress here falls directly on the schools. We must take it that the young will demand of us what they need in quality of relationship. As they "go off" their parents it becomes pronounced but it is a continual demand they make anyway for a closer relationship and warmer involvement with adults met in schools. For the modern young, teachers must be prepared to allow closer approaches; they must not be secretive about themselves as people; they must be knowable, individual, sufficiently relaxed not to feel threatened by the emotions of the young. Incessant biographical reminiscence is not what is called for either, what is needed is merely a willingness to be seen as a whole person, not as functionary hiding behind a grill of specialist preoccupations. But the grill has been put there by teachers for the best of reasons; teachers also need to protect themselves from overexposure. They are offered large classes to manage in circumstances which forbid any authentic contact. The relationships both parties need—one in which neither is threatened by overexposure—can only be met by a new social system devised to offer both the needed opportunities and the necessary safeguards. Class teaching has to go. Whatever replaces it must be less, not more, mechanical. While it must be less threatening to the "real self" both of youngsters and of teachers, it must encourage authenticity and it must enable the learning of collaboration in groups, rather than refer problems to the weak, isolated individual.

So far I have kept the emphasis closely on what I take to be most important—the conditions needed to allow a successful search for self to be pursued throughout adolescence. If this search is discouraged or blocked we shall end with an impossible society of people too crazy or too numbed to enter into any process of generating values at all. If we find Thomson's couplet apt of very many among us, we know we are dealing with a dying society. It is already true of too many that:

> Like cats in airpumps to subsist we strive
> On joys too thin to keep the soul alive.

(The image is one of cats subjected to experimental curiosity in vacuum jars.) But another important part of the present for our youngsters is the future they are forecasting for themselves, a vision of the roles they think they will be called upon to play in a predictable lifetime. The pattern men could once rely on—preparation for a career, entry to it, marriage, continuity of that career until retirement—certainly is not the predictable future. We don't know what will replace it except that it is likely to demand great resilience and more sophistication than the old pattern demanded. The likelihood is that the young need preparation for opportunities which to the unprepared will seem more like dangers. Forewarned is not forearmed in this case; when we perceive chances as threats, we respond to them with a hostility which destroys those chances and to that extent we are crippled inventors of our fate. In a world where technical inventiveness has outrun social daring to the point where there is no discernible match between them, we are playing our young false if we ask them *not* to be revolutionary. They will very much need to be welcomers of change, reasonably optimistic people who can believe in a human capacity to control change. Those who cannot welcome change will of course resist it, having no faith in any possibility of a good outcome.

This increases the strength of the demand for a profound change in the level of involvement in social invention allowed to the young while they are still at school and raises the matter of the content of education which I shall discuss elsewhere. It is the implications for the school social system that concern me here. Broadly grouping all the immediate needs and needs for preparation so far identified, we can see more clearly the size of the challenge to our ingenuity. What set up can we design which will simultaneously meet the need to

1. make far more choices in areas of learning predictedly relevant to the young's expected future
2. rehearse at an earlier age more nearly *modern* adult behaviors
3. enjoy more overtly personal relations with teachers?

This of course does not exhaust the list of needs met poorly if at all by our present system. An especially important fourth one is the need to enter more energetically into learning situations and question the validity and relevance of problems and answers offered. One of the most marked features of our times is an increasing recognition of the tentativeness of all knowledge and the speed with which items of knowledge become obsolete.

Insofar as teaching is trading in knowledge, teachers are the most vulnerable group. We are not involved in a five-year plan to replace all the old lamps of learning with new ones which will shine more brightly (that would be a relatively easy task) but in evaluating a steadily progressing turnover of new discoveries, a very high proportion of which are discoveries of new techniques. It is not possible for any specialist teacher honestly to think of himself as someone who has finished learning and so knows certainly what he must teach. Only the learner who accepts that he must go on learning can now safely be employed as a specialist teacher. The attitude we must adopt is exactly identical with the one we should promote in our students—an eager curiosity about the process of discovery so that having examined a question we stay awake to it with an undiminished curiosity which will make us re-examine it along with youngsters who may be exploring it for the first time. Unless we can come positively to prefer questioning and critical behavior from our students rather than inert obedience (and we know that most teachers really don't like creative awkward customers) we shall fail in simple terms of the accuracy of the information we purvey. We use information to provide a meeting ground with the young and there is no need for us to lean over backwards to try to produce some kind of information-free meeting—the young rightly expect us to know what we are talking about—but we do have to be prepared now constantly to change our perception of all information or we shall find ourselves defending as fact far too many displaced or suspect hypotheses.

A shift of emphasis is called for. The best learning is now most likely to happen where the itemized syllabus is abandoned and the distinction between teacher and learner is blurred to the point where, exploring together patterns of information new to both of them, the teacher's skill as a learner becomes apparent to the pupil and can be used as a model which need not be slavishly imitated but can be modified and elaborated. I think this has always been true and that it is from just such relationships at the research level that all of our advances have come. But this kind of collaboration should no longer be rare; it should be the basic teacher/learner relationship, the first aim, not the last. It is readily achieved in the best of our primary schools by individual teachers. In the secondary school it is harder to achieve because there an extra level of collaboration has to be introduced between the members of an interdisciplinary group of specialists.

This is not an insuperable obstacle and if the blurring of the roles of teacher and learner can be achieved, the problem of designing a style of schooling appropriate to our times becomes much more amenable.

There remains a last major need of the young which will have to be better accommodated in the new system than in the old. This is the need the young have of each other. Throughout adolescence an awareness grows in all youngsters of their membership in a group which is coming to power and taking over from its elders. However, death control, increasing the elders' retention of life and encouraging them also to attempt to retain power, has disturbed the age-old pattern, making the inevitable skirmishing more acute as it becomes more certain that the young see a world quite different from the world their elders see. We can expect it to be no less true that young people will seek in their own peer group their mates in both English senses of the word—their lovers, husbands, wives; allies and rivals; friends and enemies.

In school we need to establish not only better collaboration between the generations, but better collaboration of the young with each other. Certainly, given that their perception of the world as it is is likely to be clearer than ours, we need to collaborate with them to the point of learning from them; we have not only to avoid being seen as quislings by our own generation, but to eradicate the envy and the fear which tempts us to make too much of a bid to get in on their act, the social experiment which belongs to the young among themselves.

Very much indeed of what happens in schools now was devised to achieve such a takeover. Death control has after all been improving throughout the century of compulsory universal education and the cast iron English system of property control has made Britain more markedly than most countries a land of elders. The systematic ways devised to make underlings, clerks and cannon fodder of the young are control systems, ways of teaching them to recogize rivalries in a way useful to us rather than new ways more appropriate to them and to a humanity that by now desperately needs to find better ways of controlling its aggression than discharging it into unbridled competitiveness. The very least of the honest responses anybody can make who can be moved by recognition of what directed competition does to men (the appalling recognition of how we are led into murder which concludes Wilfrid Owen's *Strange Meeting*: "I am the enemy you killed, my friend") is "A plague on *all* your houses."

But still the most common systematic control of aggression in British secondary schools is a mollified ritualized duelling between "Houses" with sports trophies and "good conduct" marks as weapons (odd, by the way, that good conduct should shorten a prison sentence but lengthen schooling). The price the young are expected to pay for license not to *use* but simply to project and displace their aggression onto an "enemy" provided by the system, is a heavyweight kind of loyalty to the school itself as an institution. Sophisticated teenagers see through the bargain very clearly and identify the system as another piece of the law enforcement machinery. If you're not being got at through your loyalty to the school, pressure will be brought to bear on you by your peers in the smaller group to which you have been arbitrarily assigned, who will lose face if they don't succeed in making you toe the line. The accepters, the easily nobbled and easily led rather humourless youngsters who win most approval in this system are most truly its victims.

If we look outwards to adventure playgrounds or to careful surveys of peer groups in their normal uncontrolled habitat (such as Peter Wilmott's *Adolescent Boys in East London*[6]) the arbitrary unnaturalness of the normal good trouble-free school becomes very clear. In adventure playgrounds the young adolescent rarely gets involved in mass activities. Boys and girls alike operate in small groups which have dealings with other small groups, and they work out a social system to achieve what all the individuals want, with property protection policed without bullying, minimal agreements never detailed into elaborated codes, a system of barter and everything needed to maintain a microsociety; and it all works very well. Adult advisers are used as advisers, not as arbitrators nor as authority. What is not so easy is to find adults who will avoid obtruding signals and demand to be used simply as advisers.

The life of the streets is much the same. Unless the young have been massing for some event which is to some adults' commercial advantage and have been manipulated into hysteria, life goes on in small groups; gangs are uncommon; the depressed, usually visibly immature kids obviously seeking shelter rather than fulfilment in group membership, look for trouble of the kind none of them could cope with alone; most do not. All at some time go through a period of breaking away stress at home which their friends understand and share with them and discuss in a rambling way which enables the problem not only to be placed but to wear itself out. These discussions can reach levels of understanding and generosity unheard of in school discussions steered by a teacher towards some conclusion. (An honorable exception of unsteered discussion in a girls' school is reported and analyzed by James Britton.[7]) Most youngsters find all the help they need in the small groups they make for themselves and the group dissolves (remaining friends) when courting a partner begins in earnest.

What of those who don't succeed in helping each other in this way? I feel that the worst of their troubles is not their inability to seek help from adults, but the way in which they exclude themselves from the peer group. A readiness to bring to us the worries that would normally be consumed among themselves may in fact be a danger signal. Many of these are "good" youngsters who seem to be getting on well with their schooling. Since we do not ask them to help each other in school, we don't notice that they can't. The most lasting help that can be given is to help the dropouts join humanity and discover the values of diversity rather than offer a timid conformity.

On several counts we should be seeking to help the young exploit their natural groupings better. If such groupings become the basic way of life in as well as out of school, many quarrels that arise at present will be eliminated. We can help many more of the young to join their generation and we can shelter this vitally necessary activity, the need of the young to mull things over at leisure and in privacy, from the erosion it is likely to suffer as public space becomes even more crowded and susceptible to control than it already is.

There is already some difficulty here. Most of our young are *urban* youngsters. The restlessness of the young has a long history but ours is a tidy society which is not very tolerant of restlessness, and the urban environment of most countries offers no richer a public life than villages once did. Even in London public transport collapses at an early hour and militates against the nocturnal living all youngsters seem to find attractive, perhaps because they need to be with their peers for hours on end and can begin to do so only after the tedium of the day has worn off and most adults have retired. There may also be for many in staying up late an element of putting off the disappointment of going to bed alone.

You can see this quarrel of adult and adolescent purposes most clearly in summer in the centre of London or at seaside resorts, both of which advertise heavily to draw youngsters in and relieve them of their cash and yet offer no suitable very cheap accommodation where they may stay in groups overnight, nor public transport to get them home in the early hours. The resorts lock up and empty their tills at an hour which they find convenient. Fagged out, frustrated and rightly resentful, the young may well squabble among themselves, unleash their anger in vandalism, or become troublesome to the unfortunate policemen who are charged to prevent them from sleeping on the beaches or in the parks.

It would be better to accept wherever we can (and we certainly can in schools) the need the young have of each other, and to accept that it is stronger than any need they have of us. Accept that they have a persistent desire to "live in the group," to avoid those aspects of individualism which are more curse than blessing, and encourage it as a natural solution to their urge to rehearse and then claim full adulthood. We should give houseroom in every possible way to the dialogue of the group (not Socratic dialogue) with all the jockeying, jostling and thrashing about of values it entails. The aggressive drive shown in their apparently least controlled strivings is good and expresses the desire to live fully. We must welcome this aggression if we wish it not to be antisocial, and not to be turned inward to tear apart the growing identity. By welcoming all their achievements, their overcoming of barriers as individuals and as groups, we support the young and their strivings to create a society and to generate values.

In schools this means that we must do two things. We must welcome a much greater repertoire of activities and recognize them as important kinds of learning. And we must change the basis on which we let them group, eliminating mass groups which can be continually supervised and instituting instead much more small-group activity which cannot. This we will do if we value the dialogue within groups as highly as the dissertation with teachers. The tensions which build up in controlling the traffic of young people progressing *en masse* from classroom to classroom where authenticity and dialogue are both denied, are destructive both for teachers and youngsters and militate against any kind of learning.

Finally some words of warning. I have talked all along as if the aim of the young is to free themselves of adult guidance by inventing social controls of their own, with or without adult collaboration. I do indeed think this and also that if the impulse to do so were not inborn nobody would ever learn anything; no amount of conditioning can account for man's sociability; no amount of learning theory will discover anywhere but in the sociable impulse any motive for learning.

But my account of things will certainly seem to contradict all that people (especially teachers) have always said about the human need for security. I would say that the term security is not only too vague to be useful, but that it contains dangerously hostile overtones. The most evil men to be found in any society are the agents of the security forces. Whatever need of security people have nowadays is contained in a primary need of sensual enjoyment, the pleasing realities of the body and of *authenticity* of relationships.

But there are real difficulties for adults who are given an arbitrary relationship with the young as teachers are. We have inherited a social system of schools which depends on nonauthentic relationships and the most popular view of our job is still the version which sees us as "initiating the young into various realms of knowledge."

I have suggested that the nature of the young and of the world as it is now makes nonsense both of the system and of what most people still see as our task. The dominant style of secondary schooling is still the one devised by teachers creating a relationship appropriate as they saw it to pubertal adolescents, not to mid-adolescents. The traditions still in play are those which were established with an under-fourteen school population which matured later than the present generation does. It is an unfortunate effect of the defensiveness of childhood in our civilization that a great deal is kept secret from childhood, that sorrows, pains and the normalities of growth, and especially of sexuality, are made secret. There is no preparation for puberty, no ritual to welcome its onset, no change in the public lifestyle initiated by it. In the initial stages of adolescence the young are left alone with the knowledge of what is happening to them; they are covertly encouraged to keep it a secret from their elders who have kept so much secret from them. Perturbed and perhaps even frightened by all this and uncertain whether it represents a loss or a gain, many of them seek with an exaggerated urgency reassurance from fixed routines. They may show it in an eagerness to work at monotonous tasks; the marked spontaneity in their art may disappear; they develop obsessional traits, becoming fanatically tidy collectors; and they may openly seek from adults a firmness of detailed control. This control rapidly becomes irksome as growth and the new reality of sexuality become familiar. Then the apron strings to which they clung become halters and the will grows to be selfdirected, to earn social respect of the kind adults have, and by earning that to earn also the right to protect a territory of social power in which satisfaction of the sociable impulse and of the mating drive can be legitimately achieved.

How should this need for control be interpreted and met?

Taking it that the demand made on adults is part of a line of development which ends in joint selfcontrol and control of social situations, I cannot accept the view that rigid routine control is preferable to collaboration with teachers who offer leadership only at those times when they see it is needed (given that they will be looking out for those times). To encourage youngsters to rely on routine is to make matters worse later on. If we see that it is not our control of them that they really want, but our help in establishing their own control of surprising impulses in themselves, the help we will give will be collaboration, evidence of our care for them and evidence of the selfcertainty we ourselves have, rather than direction. They know the task of living is their own. They do not, except at rare moments of panic, want us to undertake the task for them, but to help them undertake it. We cannot live someone else's life nor the lives of our children for them. The consistency they do need from us is not a comprehensive rigidity, but a consistently flexible awareness of what they are trying to cope with.

It is even more dangerous to impose rigid routine on mid-adolescents whose energies are bent on the discovery of a competent self. To concentrate on other matters which do not seem to (and indeed don't) bear at all on the deepest central concerns of life becomes at times almost unbearably difficult and at high tides of feeling utterly impossible. The drab order of a subject timetable and days divided by measures of mechanical time are just about the least appropriate setting for the complexities of the tide of adolescent feeling with its weird fluctuations of energy and sudden flaring or withdrawal of interest. The imposed attention we invite adolescents to produce and devote to a list of topics wider, more scattered and more itemized than at any other time of life, may be repellent because it hits, symbolically, on sore spots (as when foundlings worrying about their lack of a personal family past find it impossible to cope with history) or it may be refused simply because the topics feel irrelevant. Should we be surprised that far, far more of the forced feast we set before the young in our secondary schools is rejected than accepted?

On any one day there may be in any adolescent mind a very

heated preoccupation with the vicissitudes of an intimate relationship, an ephemeral but urgent love, or a heightened touchiness with a parent, burning away internally the high energies we expect the young to have, and making the youngster appear flaccid, listless—the kind of behavior we mostly call laziness. In these circumstances teacher may teach till teacher is blue in the face and in spirit too. Psyche has her own priorities—those of immediate living—and those priorities are the realities of the young. It is easy to be patient when your impulses are weak and easy then to think that others should be patient too. It is not easy for adolescents to channel their attention. Our denial of personal rhythms, of personal styles of learning which begin more markedly to emerge with the building of identity, and our failure to allow for moods which may be transitory or persistent are responsible for most of our failures to help adolescents towards more energetic and effective learning. We offer the wrong information at the wrong times in the wrong way in poor conditions. The formal classroom arrangement and the timetabled day are containers as damaging to the young as a cage is to a tiger. In the cage the tiger will be quiet, denied the challenges which call forth its tigerish behavior. It makes a nice specimen—but it isn't really a tiger any more. Nor are our young anything like what human beings could be, if allowed to learn within a system which is itself experimental, that life is not a game to be played successfully by learning and following unalterable rules but rather a matter of identifying and exploiting the constraints which affect us as organisms in an energetic universe.

We have perhaps had our system of education in Britain too long. We have tended to boast of it. But I think it likely that what Norbert Wiener had to say of the rest of our system is even more true of our education:

> England was the first country to go through a fullscale industrial revolution; and from this early age it inherited the narrow gauge of its railways, the heavy investment of its cotton mills in obsolete equipment, and the limitations of its social system, which have made the cumulative needs

of the present day into an overwhelming emergency, only to be met by what amounts to a social and industrial revolution. All this is taking place while the newest countries to industrialize are able to enjoy the latest, most economical equipment; are able to construct an adequate system of railroads to carry the goods on economically sized cars; and in general are able to live in the present day rather than in that of a century ago.[8]

But we must be very guarded to see that we do not replace a bad system by another which makes just the same mistakes in a disguised form. The bad system came from a very inventive age which failed to protect man from his own powers. Dickens described it perfectly in *Hard Times*. Our age is even more inventive but this time we must build in disorder, and design the new system on the humble human scale. Spontaneity is not plannable, nor is genuine care. It needs to incorporate the concern expressed by Bruno Bettelheim and defend

> . . . the lassitudinous society which I'm committed to. All new inventions you're welcome to. I'm interested only in rediscovering those things that have been rediscovered for thousands of years. I think the Faustian emphasis on the absolutely new, on that which has never existed before, is the modern American disease and something which we would be much happier without.[9]

Summary

1. The whole pattern of acquisition of roles in society is undergoing a change and some roles will be achieved younger while prolongation of education will defer entry into full time work. The variety of work undertaken by people in a lifetime will be greater. The ability to enjoy change and to share the generation of new values is the trait that now demands most to be supported in adolescence.
2. The nature of families is changing. Finer standards of

personal relations are called for as all the centralizing forces which go with rapidly increasing population endanger the authenticity of relationships. Authenticity of relationship in schools becomes more important. Schooling needs to be more overtly and directly personal.

3. A special feature of changes in family, taken with the instability of contact with other adults in the community, is making adolescents refer their need for personal knowledge of adults more and more to their teachers. A schooling system which masks the teacher and frustrates frank dialogue with pupils makes it more difficult for the young to achieve a valid personality.

4. Success in life at all points in society will depend more more than hitherto on personal resilience in facing a continuing demand to learn both new techniques and new relationships. We can no longer afford merely to pay lip service to the need to make learning how to learn the core of curriculum. Nothing less can cope with the turnover of new ideas which will continue.

5. The direct, overt, or symbolic relevance of topics under review to urgent personal needs and concerns determines how much attention an adolescent can pay to the topic. Class teaching procedures are the least likely to succeed as learning situations for adolescents and devising syllabuses is an inadequate way of deciding what they should be learning.

6. To use their aggression well the young need a social system in which to learn, the one they produce for themselves where they are free to do so. This allows them regularly to experience success both as individuals and as members of small authentic groups.

7. The young need to share each other's experience and this is a need that should be as readily fulfilled in schools as elsewhere.

8. These needs are the common needs of all our youngsters, not of any specially privileged or underprivileged group. Some of them are not met at all by our present system of secondary schooling and the others are very poorly met. Radical changes are therefore called for.

Changes in Adolescence

References

1. Claude Lévi-Strauss, in G. Charbonnier, *Conversations with Claude Lévi-Strauss* (Cape Editions, 1969; Grossman, 1969).
2. Ian Taylor, *"Hooligans: Soccer's Resistance Movement,"* in *New Society* (August 7, 1969).
3. Charity James, in conversation.
4. Jonathan Kozol, *Death at an Early Age* (Houghton Mifflin, 1967; Penguin, 1968).
5. See note 4 above.
6. Peter Willmott, *Adolescent Boys in East London* (Routledge, 1966; Humanities Press, 1966).
7. James Britton, "Talking to Learn," in *Language, the Learner and the School* (Penguin, 1969).
8. Norbert Wiener, *The Human Use of Human Beings* (Houghton Mifflin, 1954; Sphere Books, 1968).
9. Bruno Bettelheim, commenting at a conference on Utopias, reported by Tim Matthews in *New Society* (August 7, 1969).

CHAPTER 3

Counting People In—or Out?

I suppose one of the people I should acknowledge as a source of this book is the secondary modern school pupil who insisted on leaving at fifteen because "You people are fine and I like you, but you haven't taught me anything I wouldn't have learned anyway just by growing up." Faced with such a challenge, I for one could no longer go on believing (especially when this young man, released from schooling, showed extraordinary brilliance and subtlety in carving out a career for himself) that my teaching was the cause of youngsters' learning. "I know, and I teach what I know, and then the pupil knows; and because I have taught him, he has learned." This is about the strength of the learning theory most teachers operate with, looking for some significance in the part they play in the lives of the young. They are not of course unsupported in this view by the many hack psychologists who have applied themselves to justification of the system as it stands. Educational psychology is over ready for the kind of explosion that has recently happened in zoology at the insistence of the ethologists who ask first of any animal's behavior how much of it belongs to its adaptation to its *social* field, i.e. how it learns to belong to its species.

To try to begin to discover what actually happens in our

schools, we must begin by asking not what happens between the teacher and the pupil, but how all the people there, through their perception of the expectations others have of them, influence each other.

Our educational system is still fundamentally selective in its purpose and this purpose is expressed in the energy and the frequency with which we sort out the sheep from the goats, the sheer repetition of signals of selection or rejection, inclusion or exclusion. One motive for this is provided by our economy, the division of labor organization of our society's productive systems. But this motive is never clearly admitted since it so obviously does not entirely account for our educational practice. The other motive has no economic rationale. Those of us who feel violent hostility to it are prone just to call it snobbish, but it would be better described, neutrally, as inertial. People in the top reaches of a hierarchy recruit to the middle reaches people who will help to maintain the status quo. The system attracts most those adults who enjoyed the system when they were children. The children of course have no choice in the matter; entry to the system is compulsory for them.

The educational system long ago lost any legitimate claim to efficiency in the division of labor business. In areas where there is no supply of adequately educated people to learn modern trades, "inadequately educated" people do it and do it well as Professor Drucker demonstrates.

> The jobs that in Ontario are being filled by high school graduates, preferably with one or two years of college, are staffed by the same employer . . . with junior high school graduates in Quebec. They are paid quite differently; yet there is not much difference in the jobs they do or in their productivity.
>
> The direct cause of the upgrading of jobs is, in other words, the upgrading of the educational level of the entrant into the labour force. The longer he or she stays in school, the more education will be required for entrance into a given job or occupation.[1]

So this aspect of education has to be explained as inertial too, a matter of maintaining values by making people equate their success in schools with their life potential. I would not suggest that we perform a deliberate confidence trick on the youngsters we persuade to stay in our schools to enhance their career prospects. In effect, we are paid not for our work but for our performance in school and the fact that we did not drop out. Ontario graduates are paid more than Quebec junior high school workers for the same work. We do our youngsters no disservice in pointing this out because this differential does occur in all industrial societies. What we should stop pretending is that the *content* of schooling has any direct relationship to later work, or that it directly influences later ability to master all that is needed for any trade. Systems analysis and the threat of automation are rapidly demythologizing our descriptions of the skill needed for all kinds of work anyway, but of course all employers tend to think far more is required than is in fact necessary to the job, so they go for "the educated man." It doesn't improve production but it does do something for the status of your business.

This by the way is a transitory stage. More and more work can be automated at all levels; the computer imitates brains, not hands, and it has language of a kind and can communicate. When it comes to the crunch and the choice is not between educated and uneducated people, but between man and machine, machines will be employed. We cannot tell how long this phase will last but it is a safe prediction that the most entrenched foundation of competition in education is really threatened now. If competition is to be maintained, it must be for its own sake and because it is held to be good in itself. In that case we must abandon our pretensions that our society is democratic since we could hardly justify antidemocratic practices in a democratic society on any grounds other than those of necessary evil expediency. If schooling is to assist in socialization of the young it must be *democratic* socialization. If it is to help identify and develop talent, and the talent is *not* to be specifically matched to the state of the labor market, the talents to be sought are those of a generally inventive kind and it is especially important that they should be talents which can be democratically employed.

The *genuine* relationship which exists between schooling and division of labor is the one revealed by Anthony Sampson, which is anything but democratic:

> The city is traditional; much of it is run on the "fagging system" . . . of employing young men, often intelligent and expensively educated, at menial tasks for several years, copying transfers, writing in ledgers, or checking figures. The docile "public school proletariat" are employed on jobs which for some years may need no part of their expensive education except simple arithmetic . . . . The justification is that the city is based on *trust* . . . . The speed of the city's operations depends on the acceptance of verbal promises . . . . This quick trust, it is argued, depends on knowing to whom or what kind of person you are talking—knowing he is "one of us."[2]

This is precisely the case. If during the century of universal compulsory education which is just ending, our schools served any democratic purposes it was certainly not by intent. The introduction of the state grammar schools may have trained more of us to lead the masses but I would not call that democratic. Are the attitudes to school and children represented in the following extracts from a village school log book significantly different from the attitudes you would find expressed by teachers in relaxed conversation about their work now? There are no log books and of course no headteacher would use this language in the Governor's report but that isn't the point. The point is that what happens in schools and the day to day preoccupations of teachers seem to have changed remarkably little.

> The children have been most unruly, so I attended to discipline. Spoke to infants' room teacher about being a good disciplinarian on Wednesday. This she evidently resented for she sulked for nearly ten minutes. I gave a lesson on The Hedgehog, and taught Standard III The

Division of Factors. Cautioned five children not to go stone picking in school hours. Took word building with upper standards . . . . The four children who have obtained their Labour Certificate have taken advantage of it and left school.

(next year) The glorious reign of Queen Victoria, the Year of Jubilee . . . was celebrated. The greatest progress in popular education was made during this last half century. Still it is very defective, especially in this school.

Had cause to speak to provisional teacher about her striking and shaking the children. Colonel Manvers visited the school and cautioned PT. Infants simply do as they like in her presence.[3]

Despite the fact that nowadays many infant class teachers would be pleased if the children really did as they liked, and that many teachers in our primary schools would read these records as those of a foreign world, they seem to me to picture clearly enough the values of the modern secondary school. Teachers give lessons quite confident of their rightness (I guess the children knew more than the headmistress about hedgehogs). Physical punishment is not unknown but it is the head's ritualized prerogative. Teachers still believe in progress and in perfectability and will go on applying the system until it works, while admitting it doesn't yet. They can call on an outside authority and the thing that worries them most is controlling the children.

The children were not in those days actually required to wear uniform and it took pretty persistent policing to get many of them to school at all. Fortunately, the excellent study in depth of village life which I have been quoting tells us what the children remembered of their schooling, and what happened to those who "took advantage of their Labour Certificate" which guaranteed they were sufficiently educated to be employable:

Father took my brother and myself to his new employer and twizzling me round so that I could be seen said, "Here's a good strong boy. I want 4s 6d a week for him."

"We'll see about that at the end of the week," said the farmer.[4]

For such a future, such an education was completely apt. But it was apt not because of any patterns of cognitive information the boy had picked up, nor because of any methods of learning he had been invited or driven to pay conscious attention to, but because of the strength with which it reinforced all the forces driving him to obey and to accept what others more favored or more powerful might do to him. It is at this level that educational systems have their most powerful effects and it is at this level that we must examine our educational system. Men do not become chattels until they have become sufficiently dispirited. If the system works well enough they can be brought to believe, dispiritedly, that they have been inspired. The system can still prove an undoing for others whose spirit cannot be broken. These others may do well but care not at all for their fellows; they may become alienated and badly pervert public policies if they attain power as many of them do; they may join the system and become its creature rather than their own as many more do; they may habituate themselves to struggling without expecting to win and be defused by learning only to explode, without acquiring any strategies which might enable them to alter things.

I am not arguing that our system is a conscious, designed product of an intention to immobilize the innate talents of most people in order to maintain the balance of power in society. I am suggesting that, without conscious intent, the system and the pattern of relationships reflected exactly the dominant values of the society which first produced it by legislation (building of course on such system as there already was) and that there have been no radical changes in the system since then. I am also suggesting that we are capable of designing systems deliberately, and that any changes we make in future should be through redesigning systems as a whole and not just tinkering with bits of the obsolete machinery.

I see the system we have as one which does not succeed in

doing what most people say it is intended to do or what indeed they think it does do. Moreover as I have said I think it damages most of the people who go through it. I admit to believing in the ingenuity of my species, and to thinking that none of us is ever really stretched—a dreadful Procrustean image, but I may as well take this sideswipe at the defenders of our selective grammar schools using their own language. To make so little of the talents of the cleverest seems to me shameful.

Our grammar schools operate in just the same way as other secondary schools. There is a common form of secondary schooling, a common structure to the school day, a common system of relationships, all of which leads to calling C streamers dim or unteachable whatever school they are in and whatever their measured intelligence is supposed to be. The school, whatever its population, is likely to be

1. ranked (unofficially) somewhere in a national or local hierarchy
2. organized on only two sets of dominant decisions: (a) how much time is to be spent by each class in studying each subject thought appropriate for it, the appropriateness being almost entirely traditionally determined; (b) distribution of teachers to teach these subjects at the ordained times in spaces which may be especially equipped for the purpose or may not
3. streamed in homogeneous groups of fixed composition and numbering around thirty, the grouping being determined by records of earlier school performance which are regarded as reliable indicators of ability
4. highly authoritarian in all relationships as a result both of the fact that (a) there is a dominant tradition of such relationships in schools, and (b) a structure like the one I have outlined *has* to be authoritarian in that it allows for only a few rare, crude decisions to be made on poor evidence by few of the people (usually a caucus of teachers supporting the head) enclosed in the structure.

We are used to accepting this structure as the right one. But once any part of it (such as streaming) gives way under pressure of evidence of its harmful effects on the young, the whole structure collapses. It turns out to have been all along the container of a systematic limiting of talent achieved by guaranteeing a massive experience of failure in conditions where alienation (enforced isolation from your fellows) is always the order of the day.

The difference between structures and systems which interests me here (one which I know to have been meaningless for years now in physics and biochemistry and all the sports bred between them) is this: a structure can be easily envisaged as an interlocking of separable parts; a system can barely be envisaged at all, but has to be apprehended as an interplay of processes. Try imagining a viscous jigsaw puzzle with the pieces melting in your hands, and you will understand the difficulty. Again we are running into part of our heritage we have to reject, which is the habit of relying on a rigid mechanical image to see how things work. What we can imagine as a structure we can construct or reconstruct by a process of assembling parts and putting them together. We can rearrange the hierarchy; we can redefine the subjects and rethink their appropriateness; we can constitute groups differently; we can revise teaching method in the light of laboratory experiments in new techniques of instruction. Put these together and what will we get? The system as before. We shall still be thinking of learning as a series of events, of knowledge collecting instead of knowing, and we shall produce the same old inauthentic relationships.

Following George Alexander Kelly[5] I take it that the only meaningful way to see people is as processes, speaking psychologically, and speaking biologically as processes in a system of energy exchange. A man is a creature moving in ways he has learned, but may alter, among constraints both the nature and the pattern of which affect him only through the meanings he gives them. They are real enough but it is our interpretation of them we respond to and we live by exploiting them in the light of our interpretation, which remains primarily emotional however clever we may be. Our vision of everything beyond ourselves (even where we locate our "edges") is highly, individually personal, however much of it may be shared with others and however strongly or weakly we feel the bidding of our sociable impulse to share visions. The sharing, however many ways of sharing there may be, is at the heart of human learning, the acquisition of the very complex habits which enable us to identify, alter our view of, and exploit constraints. Our very personal view of others and of our relationship with them as constraints we can exploit or as constraints not to be meddled with does more than anything else to shape our lives.

At this most radical level a social system is not a map of traffic routes between social institutions or separable parts of a social structure. It is rather a system of *interpersonal* relations mediated by agreements or approximations of personal visions of constraints.

This is tough going. But when the framework collapses or shifts in the way I described in my first two chapters, things which once seemed to be settled outside us are referred back to us and there is a genuine demand for new relationships, as they are the only way out of alienation. Much as we may all nostalgically lust after old certainties (and it would surprise me very much to meet anybody who doesn't at times) we have now to attend quite urgently to the quality of our sharing at a personal level and our vision of how things are. Both dialogue and shared exploratory action must be reinstituted as the centre of the educational process.

It is precisely this which is excluded by the structure we are using. The secondary school at present is its timetable, which usually looks tidy and efficient, but in fact, like most details of procedure in our classrooms, masks massive failure. This in fact is what makes me feel without reservation that little worth preserving will be lost if we reorganize schools completely to regain authenticity of relationships, a yield I know we can reap only at the cost of abandoning the timetable and making decisions of another kind, ordered in another way. What we should not allow to stand in the way of making such sweeping changes is the fear that we shall somehow lose knowledge from our communities, that our "heritage of learning" will seep away. There is no reason to think and every reason to doubt that learning is as difficult as our schools make it seem. One of the most vicious effects of a universally compulsory system of education, which is at the same time geared only for selection, has been to set up the whole process as an obstacle race (which lasts not for the measured minutes used in laboratory conditioning experiments, but for years and years). Learning has been *made* difficult and we have come to think of difficulty as inherent in knowledge rather than as being put in our way by the system which seems to be offering knowledge to us. To think otherwise is after all to be forced to a bitter criticism of our teachers which would be difficult to maintain over all those years; and we start off very young, aware of needing adult guidance, in a very weak position.

This deception is propagated through teaching subjects to classes. All the pupils are expected to attend to the same information in the same way at the same time. The teacher is too busy imparting or steering information to see what individuals are up to. He must also try to take away evidence of performance with him for examination, evidence which must be strictly limited in order to be manageable. It is such a minute fragment of what has been going on in all those minds that it provides no worthwhile evidence and is simply irrelevant to the actual process. But it is manageable and recordable if what is demanded on paper is non-controversial and can be regarded as so many items of right or wrong understanding of the message given (or rather of a little part of it). We never in fact set questions on more than ten per cent of any syllabus. The rest may be regarded as waste. A high score on the little we do inefficiently examine is accepted and praised as good performance. The results are that success is paltry and can often be achieved just by ticking over.

It can be dangerous in fact really to think about what a teacher is saying—you may not only hear too much, you may try to reproduce it and end up being wrong instead of right. The lessons always tend to be reduced to little encapsulated question and answer rituals that have nothing at all to do with thinking. The situation exists for its own sake and I'm afraid my observations suggest that *most* of the time anybody spends in our secondary schools is spent in just such rituals where the line between success and failure is haphazardly drawn. But most youngsters, like most teachers, do take all this nonsense seriously. After all it is an important part of their lives. The fact that they are legally required to suffer it indicates that it is a matter of great social importance. They are there getting what they can out of the relationship. They can't cut off completely and it deeply affects their vision and interpretation of constraints—not only the constraints of school either.

The effects on the teachers are equally damaging. Most secondary schools (at least in the south of England) are staffed with a teacher for every eighteen pupils, yet classes are commonly in the upper thirties. Where does the slack go? Into fulfilling the requirements of the elegantly rococo bureaucracy which houses and channels the worthless records of a little of what happened in the classroom and all the memorandized minutiae of traffic and personnel control.

To picture the disparity between what actually happens and what is supposed to happen in our secondary schools would take a book in itself. Most of my readers will be familiar with it, but I would suggest to any teacher in such a school that it would be worthwhile to try an experiment. Pair with another teacher in another such school. Spend at least one day as a pupil following an actual pupil's daily timetable and examine carefully every scrap of your paired colleague's paper work for a month. How much of either experience will you find relevant to anything but the closed system of that school? Only insofar as there might be an improvement in the handling of language which would not have been achieved just by growing up, does this schooling contribute anything positive to the lives of the people who have been put through the mill.

At this point—if not many, many pages back—I am sure many readers will be muttering that I am being obdurately unrealistic, not because they think the system unchangeable or even have much fondness for it but because it is so clear that whatever we are trying to teach, some children have an aptitude for this, some for that, and some it seems for hardly anything that goes on in school or in life either come to that.

The point is we never *do* come to that. We make an offer of *subjects*, not of *problems*. If we ever come round to genuine

human problems, questions of what humanity should be trying
to do, it is by way of subjects and an attempt to demonstrate
the relevance of these subjects. Approaching it from that angle
the problems are cut and dried before we start—we only tackle
problems which we think the subject has already solved and
those aren't problems at all. We are excluding the children from
genuine problems just as we exclude them from genuine
decisions. Now I would say *that* is being unrealistic. Aptitude
for what is being offered is important only when the offering is
varied enough to cater for every kind of aptitude. There are
only three important basic aptitudes, each of a very general
kind; aptitude to make and to see relationships; aptitude to use
language; aptitude for sound, nonhallucinatory perceptions (but
an additional aptitude for surviving hallucinations may be an
extra benefit). Without these you're sunk. With them, given that
you have not been put off and have a genuine need to use
knowledge (it may be a need for something to play with, to be
amused by—just as potent as any work need) there is certainly
no "knowledge" found in A level certificate examinations that
is beyond the reach of very ordinary youngsters. (I cite A rather
than O level because it's less mumbojumbo ridden. The
questions put begin to be complex enough to be worth
answering.)

  The proliferation of separate subjects and the improvement in
the supply of subject specialist teachers are not of course
responsible for the streaming of youngsters. That has to be
explained by the view a selective system generates in those who
are serving it. Schools exist to pick out those who can and bring
them on. If the cost is that we have to prove to the others that
they can't, well they can't can they so what's the damage? But
if I reverse the usual question and say that it isn't success that
needs explaining, but failure; or rather insist (very reasonably)
that learning goes on all the time and that those the teacher says
succeed are learning what the teacher wants them to, and the
others are learning something else—a social message about
themselves—and that *this* is the behavior that needs explaining
because youngsters always please teachers if they can, what
then?

Usually I am given the technical runaround with talk of attention spans, memory spans, perseverance factor, ability to concentrate, measurements of squint and focus. In plain staffroom language it comes down to "Some kids have what it takes and some don't. Remedial kids are born dim, middle stream kids are bone idle or feckless, and the top stream will have to pull its socks up or they'll get poor grades in the exam."

These attitudes, a simple belief (or a hunger to believe) in some sort of innate intelligence, a fixed measured injected dose of "withitability" which produces streaming by nature, I have found lurking within the overt egalitarianism of many of the most "liberal" teachers I have met. The fact that many people find things that interest us boring or even repulsive is apparently too simple to be grasped by teachers. We insist that differences in interest must represent differences in cleverness. None of us can see what is so difficult to grasp in ideas we ourselves hold without difficulty so we read all struggles as signs of something lacking in the child, an absence of something necessary to understanding. We are not equipped to look into a youngster's mind or subtly sift his history to see where he was put off, and we act as if we thought that human beings could have inherited quite different instinctual gifts.

I am not prepared to believe that human beings receive different kinds of instincts from each other nor that the instinctual will to learn, which is so clearly present in all human infants, is so unlike the instinctual inheritance of all other creatures as to grow "naturally" weaker as we age. We are not, I think, born like rockets, with a first firing stage which just drops off after giving us an initial boost. If curiosity dwindles, the explanation must be sought in constellations of experiences which sap selfconfidence, in the learning of "proper limits" beyond which the individual feels he must not question. All we know of human infancy, the dispiriting effects of separation anxiety, animal life, and commonsense commonplace observation indicate that our learning happens within relationships with other people. There would be no development of ideas at all in someone who had *never* exchanged ideas with others. Helen Keller is a handy example of this. The speechless, blind, utterly isolated child needed a warm, reassuring relationship to receive the gift of language and having that had almost no limits.

Readiness to learn is readiness to learn collaboratively. Language has been shaped collaboratively and still is. The artists who make the most definitive uses of it are people who have a very strong sense of audience indeed, who write both to understand themselves and to involve others in that understanding. And it is language, not the senses nor the layout of synaptic pathways, which organizes human perceptions. It may well have its own characteristics, shapes and limits applying to all human languages alike, but then there is a basic shape and pattern to all human relationships. Underlying all hierarchies, all horn locking, all ranking and wrangling there is always the basic question of whether we are IN or OUT. Am I loved and/or respected here? If I am, what goes here goes for me too and what these people master, I can.

I am oversimplifying grossly in search of the fundamental, which is (for the purpose of thinking about schools) that barriers imposed by us on any child's entry into collaboration with his fellows or with us explain "failures to learn" well enough. But of course it is the child's own view of the situation which determines whether there are any barriers and no two people ever see any situation identically.

These considerations, however, give me the first tests to apply to any learning situation. Is collaboration possible? Is any genuine dialogue possible? Who is working with whom? Can they talk things out? If people are expected to occupy an enclosed space together and ignore each other, the greatest of all possible barriers to learning has already been erected.

But of course even in such a hostile situation we are learning. You cannot be awake and not be learning. As Kelly puts it:

The problem of learning is not merely one of determining how *many* or what kinds of reinforcement fix a response, or how many nonreinforcements extinguish it, but rather how does the subject phrase the experience, what recurrent themes does he hear, what movements does he define, and what validation of his predictions does he reap? When a subject fails to meet the experimenter's expectations, it may be inappropriate to say that "he has not learned"; rather one might say that what the subject learned was not what the experimenter expected him to learn. If we are to have a productive science of psychology, let us put the burden of discovery on the experimenter rather than on the subject. Let the experimenter find out what the subject is thinking about, rather than asking the subject to find out what the experimenter is thinking about.[6]

Of course we only tell people we trust what we really think. Others we tell what we think it will please them to hear. Even aversion therapy it seems, according to a *New Society* report by Dr. Eysenck, only works where the subject understands the therapeutic intention of the psychiatrist and collaborates in the treatment.[7]

But schools are not as simple as experimental cells. The way the young feel about each other is at least as important in deciding how far the youngsters will let themselves go as the way they feel about the teacher; and the teacher is seen through double vision both as a person and as "one of them." We come very readily to predict all teachers but trusting them is another matter. Indeed we *must* predict the teacher in a teacher-directed situation. This sizing up of the state of the relationship with everybody near us, and especially with the leader if there is one, goes on all the time in all of us and I take this to be instinctual, positive and ineradicable. Attention to other messages given simultaneously will always depend on these predictions. Do we need any other explanation of naughtiness in class? Frustration of the sociable impulse reinforced by the evident irrelevance of the message offered by the teacher, or the book, film, program or pipe-rack he has directed you to work on leaves you only three choices; first to work in a desultory way until the bell rings to the lowest of the low standards you know to be acceptable avoiding all difficulties; second, to abandon hope of relationship with this teacher and retreat into daydream while outwardly keeping up some automatic activity, or thirdly to reassert yourself by getting in touch with your friends some-how.

Most competent secondary school teachers, on first reading a new timetable, note immediately the occasions when they will be following a repressive colleague, knowing that they will have to adopt a style which allows for that inevitable reassertion of humanity by the pupils. If they are teachers of minority time subjects they dread these occasions, knowing, they will "get no work done" and that the syllabus just will not be covered at all that year. A head (or his deputy who is expected to be aware of these problems) tries to take this problem into account. The most common solution is to try to follow on with physical training or (alas for music and for the teacher) with music or with English.

Of course the problems are not solved that way. The main trouble with timetables is simply that they never work anyway. In our large city schools they are purely notional distributions of time to subjects and nothing more. Predictions of teachers' competence can't be made with an average annual thirty per cent staff turnover; the daily fluctuation of both staff and pupil population is ten per cent which means that one lesson in ten is taken by a teacher standing in for an absent colleague (so much for continuity, the *raison d'etre* of timetables); and of course children fall ill, or evade lessons or are otherwise employed in the school, so that continuity is even more disrupted for individuals than it is for the class. The timetable which operates perfectly, which has no inbuilt areas of immediate local decision, i.e. recognition that continuity of instruction is *not* necessary to learning at all, depends even on the weather. Time is set aside for games which are hardly ever played.

The only continuity that is meaningful for the learner is to be allowed, once he finds something worth his attention, to go on until he has mastered it, whether that takes a day, a week or a month. But if this is to achieved the old style timetable must go to be replaced by a system of local agreements, enabling teachers and children jointly to evaluate the need for time to be given to a particular phase of learning. Teachers and youngsters have to know each other much better to make such evaluations and since teachers have to seek for more agreements among themselves and have to learn *not* to rely on the head for early decisions, the quality of relationships between all parties becomes the first and not the last concern of the school. Robbed of his timetable, the school principal is not robbed of something to do but may expand the role he plays in helping his staff towards better relationships.

The second test to be applied is how open, frank and selfrevealing can all parties be? We are all reserved with people who seem to reserve themselves. The ball is at the teacher's feet. It isn't only because we trail clouds of authority that it is unfair to expect the youngsters to initiate better relationships (they do their best already) but because better relationships will only develop in a system intended to encourage them and the system is in the hands of the teachers.

The third test follows from much of what I have already said about problems of continuity of contact and authenticity of relationship. It covers the fifth part of the structure of our secondary schools, which I did not list because it works worst—all that is covered by the rather unfortunately churchy phrase "the duty of pastoral care," which covers everything from playground patrol to counselling, chatting up parents on open day, chastising delinquents, filling in employment-aptitude questionnaires, writing reports for the courts, conducting house tutorials if the school has them, or just expressing, against the odds, a genuine friendly concern for an individual youngster whose plight upsets you.

The last of these, simple uncluttered noncondescending charity, is the most difficult for a teacher to achieve in the stonily authoritarian system. We may all be born seeking a smile to respond to with warmth, love and dependence, but long before we reach adolescence we have all learned to be wary of the smile on the face of the tiger, of smug smiles, of condescending smiles, and the grins that invite nothing but compliance. Simple friendliness, for its own sake rather than as an implement of authority in a polite mood, is highly suspect in the teaching profession and youngsters too (rightly, as things stand) are wary of accepting it. They hear an axe grinding in the background, not as clearly as the women did who married King Henry, but loud enough to make them shy.

Again the fault lies in the system and not in the personalities of the people who are trying to operate it. The class teacher in the primary school who does not direct all activities but allows a good many open areas of activity can come to know the children genuinely. Even under the pressure of being expected to attend to the needs of forty or fifty children, which is the impossible task primary school teachers slog on at year after year, the kind of knowledge they have is at least much more authentic than anything most secondary school specialists ever see.

In the secondary school teachers are invited to use two quite distinct modes of knowing the young; modes which in fact cannot coexist. Inevitably the dominant mode disqualifies the other. In specialist class teaching the teacher of a majority time subject is likely to deal with 150 children a week. The clientele of a minority time subject teacher is likely to reach such extraordinary levels as 450. These are conservative estimates based on teaching thirty periods of a forty period week, allowing six periods for a majority time subject and two for a minority—I have left out any standing in for absent teachers.

Can anyone pretend to any personal knowledge of children in these circumstances? This world breaks down into three categories of child—two very small ones of goodies and baddies (say ten per cent in each) and an enormous class of nonentities. As far as the nonentities are concerned the only evidence the teacher has of their existence—let alone their abilities or even their faces—is what remains in the mark book after written work brought away from classes has been cursorily examined. And what goes into the records to which everybody refers when decisions have to be made which may profoundly affect a youngster's life, is the sum of the sums of performance in the classroom. Except that is for the goodies or baddies of whom it is known that they have resisted or helped their teachers noticeably.

If we are asked to cope with 150 people a week without knowing them, as if we were serving in a shop, we could adopt the withdrawal techniques of shop assistants. If the additional demand is made that we should *know* the customers we must, in selfdefense and to avoid overexposure, keep the contact shallow and bureaucratize it as much as possible. The resultant inauthenticity we all know. We save ourselves additionally by seeking a handful of goodies and baddies with whom we can enter into clearly defined, slightly more personal, but ritualized relationships. The result is I think that we don't really know the goodies either and certainly don't understand the baddies.

We play the same goodies/baddies/nonentities game on our colleagues too. It is the standard pattern of school relations. And this more than anything else (though the divide and conquer allowances payment system helps) goes on increasing the staff turnover rate in every school and the wastage rate of people giving up the profession altogether.

It is so glaringly obvious that we can't and don't know the youngsters we teach that most secondary schools develop a second parallel set of groupings cutting across class groupings and distribute children to teachers as house tutors, with a weekly meeting of the tutor group allowing people to "get to know each other." Much of the time allowed for this has to be consumed in policing or in the other demands of the bureaucracy.

Since tutors are usually ranged in a hierarchy under a head of house, and the house system is usually still thought of as providing "healthy competition," much more time is spent exhorting youngsters to show more interest in the exceedingly uninteresting kinds of competition approved and laid down in regulations. Problems of discipline are usually channelled through the house system too and the head of house is expected to be able to switch off at an instant's notice the role of police superintendent (used by the head to police staff as well as students) which consumes most of his time, to play instead the role of friend and counsellor. In real life some people become policemen, other people become counsellors—nobody can be both.

We have to choose between the two modes of knowing. If we genuinely believe that there is some necessary linear development to learning, that it isn't just a living process but a railroad that leads to a terminus where all is known, we must just accept timetabling as it stands and class teaching as it stands. These devices do honestly represent a belief that learning is a series of events, each of which can be performed separately with a good cumulative effect, and that all we need to know of the young we are teaching can be gathered from written evidence of these events. I do not find this belief credible and I do not think anybody would find it credible except when talking about schools. If we do want to know the youngsters we are dealing with; if we do believe that we cannot help them to learn anything without understanding them, without having a genuine sense of their personal style, we must get rid of the system and the actual organization which prevents us from knowing and understanding and build a system designed to let us know.

Summary

Points of failure

The worst shortcomings of the present system of secondary schooling are:

1. Competition within the educational system is fostered for ends which cannot be excused on the grounds of economic expediency since the demands of the labor market have only the most faint and tenuous bearing on the variety of devices of selection used at puberty or in adolescence. The chief device is the provision of selective schools (with its inevitable concomitant provision of reject schools) and streaming within schools. Of these devices the latter is more deadly.
2. The social system in schools is not mildly Victorian. Measured against other of our social institutions it is very highly authoritarian and militates strongly against any development of democratic responsibility. This system is

incorporated in normal teacher attitudes. Authoritarianism should not be confused with proneness to punish or be regarded as being present only where politeness breaks down. Authoritarian attitudes are in fact enforced on teachers, not least by their adoption of the practices necessary to maintain a pretense of efficiency for class teaching methods.

3. The use of subject specialist class teacher distribution as the basis of timetabling and thus controlling the school operates as an authoritarian conditioning device by very severely restricting the areas and incidence of decisions made by teachers and pupils alike. In large schools it is in constant disrepair and does not achieve its aim of guaranteeing continuity of learning in any subject.

4. It also results in severely overexposing teachers to student contact. This is an insuperable barrier to authenticity of human contact and reduces it to a low bureaucratic level, preventing any accurate observation of youngter's actual needs and talents.

5. Being taught mostly in classes also overexposes pupils to the point where most of their time is spent in selfconcealment and a very low level of effort, which is both a sign and cause of damage to selfesteem. The result (even where standards are held to be high by school standards) is a massive experience of failure for all parties.

6. All these conditions tend to one end—alienation—which is exactly the opposite of the socialization all parties using the system say they are trying to achieve.

Points of departure

1. Any new system must be designed with a view to the difficulties likely to be encountered on the way to implementing it which will certainly be by gradual steps. It must be phasable yet not lend itself to piecemeal random changes. Its priorities should be social rather than administrative and it should be capable of meeting these demands.

2. It should foster authenticity in knowledge and in relationships, enable teachers to know pupils and pupils to know teachers. This can only happen if most work goes on in small groups, so conditions must also be sufficiently relaxed for teachers to allow groups to work much of the time without direct supervision. Authenticity is doubly important since it is a condition for trust.

3. It must foster dialogue between pupils and collaboration sometimes with teachers, sometimes without. This also can only be achieved in small groups.

4. It must promote tackling important questions or problems which deserve to be pursued and genuinely alert the concerns of the young. Its timetabling must be highly flexible to allow the pursuit of such questions in depth and with concentration. This demands collaboration between teachers and pupils in defining the limits of such studies, and collaboration between teachers to provide interdisciplinary expertise through playing an advisory, not an instructional role, without respect for subject boundaries.

5. It must also allow teachers to retain an instructional role at times in ways which do not conflict with the pursuit of interdisciplinary enquiries at other times, but which need not be linked with them. It should indeed encourage specialization whenever and wherever youngsters show a marked disciplined bent or interest.

6. It should allow for an extension of the range of disciplines open to study without limiting the entry age to specialist subject courses and extend this to all students rather than reserve it for a few. It should normally permit part-time release to study elsewhere if the school cannot cope.

7. It should allow more rapid and expert diagnosis of both personal and educational hang ups so that help of a highly specific kind can be offered and accepted as a matter of course and not as a remedial provision in any way shameful to the recipient. Additional demands created by this requirement are very much better relations with families and with social workers of all kinds. The remedial educational

tional requirement which applies to all youngsters (since all meet stumbling blocks, however bright) will require programming and new techniques of a subtle kind.

References

1. Peter F. Drucker. "The Knowledge Society," in *New Society* (August 24, 1969).
2. Anthony Sampson, *Anatomy of Britain Today* (Hodder and Stoughton, 1965; Harper and Row, 1965).
3. Ronald Blythe, *Akenfield* (Allen Lane, The Penguin Press, 1969; Pantheon, 1970).
4. See note 3 above.
5. G. A. Kelly, *The Psychology of Personal Constructs* (Norton, 1955).
6. See note 5 above.
7. H. J. Eysenck, "Behaviour Therapy Versus Psychotherapy," in *New Society* (August 7, 1969).

CHAPTER 4

Designing a
Fourfold Curriculum

Put at its simplest, the charge against the present system is that
nobody within it can really act well; pupils can do no other
than underachieve, teachers can do no other than overdirect.
This is not an accusation of either party but it will have to be
the teachers who break a way out of the system. Most of the
parents are sold on the system as it is; most administrators are
caught up in a political crossfire and use what energy is left over
from the fantasy life of committees to worry about the
distribution of scarce money and provision of school places
rather than to promote change within schools. Education
committees contain very few people who are not in thrall to
cheap ideologies and rarely show any warm recognition of real
educational issues unless their prejudices are flouted, and much
the same seems to be true of Parliament. But this is almost as it
should be. No change of system that demands also a change of
heart can possibly come from strengthening the leadership
principle. Leaders can ban books or even, like Hitler, get us to
burn books, but they cannot help us to a better reading either
of books or of life unless they are in authentic relationship with

us. Any ground won for humanity in the system is always won by friendly alliances of teachers as seen in the local associations who joined together to form the National Association for the Teaching of English, which has achieved more in a decade than any institution set up "from the top" could achieve in a century. All associations of specialists make ground in this way; the pity is that they are not reclaiming common ground.

Pressure, criticism, recommendations and support may well come from sources outside schools, but I hope I have demonstrated that there are no aspects of curriculum which are not also aspects of relationships initiated by teachers or of the social system governing signals transmitted within the learning environment. And where any bounds are set to that environment, it will always be the teachers' own limits that set the bounds of what is proper. Wave after wave of progressive education has sunk into the sands leaving the coastline littered with interesting specimens but unaltered. The boundaries are still firm and will remain firm until teachers achieve another vision of their role and of themselves by choosing to perform an act of perception like the one George Herbert thought we have to perform to get true religious insight:

> A man who looks on glass
> On it may stay his eye,
> Or if he chooses, through it pass
> And so the heavens espye.

We must look *through* the structure to the system that sustains it; there is no other way out of the old world into the new.

Not the least of my reasons for demanding a new system capable of generating curriculum within schools is that no other approach can prevent the present structure from being overloaded until it collapses. Anthony Sampson says of the City of London that it is "never likely to collapse suddenly, with a broken mainspring; its danger is that it might, like the Hapsburg court, gradually become irrelevant to the modern world."[1] Our schooling has already passed into the phase of irrelevance and most of the attempts being made to revalidate it rely on the structure being maintained for their implementation. Good as they are in themselves, package deal schemes of integrated studies and new teaching kits for established subjects (new maths, new science, new technology, the new humanities) are all devised as closed systems prepared for handling by a class teacher; and the more of such schemes a school goes in for, the more rigidly its timetabling for class teaching is determined by the need to carry out the instructions on the packet. These packages are doomed to the same failure as earlier progressive movements by their initial, inbuilt acceptance of the system already established. They will merely be fashionable, tried and then abandoned both because they become a nuisance and because they will turn out to be unsuccessful. To be successful they demand a high tolerance of ambiguity and an openness of perception which runs counter to the demand for certitude and rectification imposed by the social system. Reworked as kits of programmed materials which do *not* depend on serial presentation within a subject syllabus for their effect, such packages would be a boon. As long as they impose timetabling on the school, they are a danger. They bring us even closer to this kind of thinking which for me would be the ultimate deterrent from wanting to get within ten miles of a school:

> Class lengths through the day may vary from twenty minutes to perhaps sixty. Not all lessons or subject areas require the same amount of time for all students. Flexible scheduling and short time modules of twenty minutes are opening new areas for improving instruction.[2]

"Short time modules"—the ultimately repulsive piece of bargaining.

But that *is* where the trends are leading us. More than a few of our own big urban secondary schools have already got their timetables into such a tangle that nobody gets any peace in the day at all. The lunch hour has become a hasty feeding time, with staggered classes and staggered dining sessions, the midday break has been cut back to as little as forty minutes, and for the teachers at least varies from day to day with teaching requirements. I don't know of a factory where workers would stand for such a persistent grind or management demand it.

Oh brave new world that has such timekeeping in it. Can we really expect that in such a clock and tannoy parcelled day Laurence Stenhouse's admirable (and admirably expressed) intentions for helping the teacher by providing new materials can be achieved? His suggestions demand of the teacher that he should know his pupils well enough to be able to

> . . . help a classroom discussion group to find its own way to an understanding of the issues at stake and should try to moderate group pressures on pupils to conform insofar as they express themselves socially rather than intellectually.[3]

The depth of the intellectual dressing may differ, but the true value shaping that goes on, where there is so much more pressure on all the individuals contained in a repulsive system to break down, is militantly conformist. New methods have no hope of attaining their objectives where the fundamental rules are those of mass hysteria.

> When a person breaks down during mystical contemplation or is broken down in mass orgiastic rallies, the faith suddenly created tends to conform to the beliefs and faith of the group or individual then in close contact with him.[4]

So we become creatures of the system, compelled to perpetuate it and this brings up the most difficult aspect of the problem of designing a new system. No social system can be expected to operate well if it has to be reinvented frequently and if all the people in it are having continually to make decisions about the system itself. Yet any new system must be very open to change. For instance the undoubted benefits of new instructional methods, given that they can be modified for collaborative rather than solitary or class teaching uses, should be rapidly assimilated. Major innovations of information or techniques in any discipline should be allowed rapidly to displace the old, and democratic decision about the conduct of the community and its work should be going on constantly. The system should be flexible enough to allow rapid change and innovation in such matters, and yet be simple to operate so that the new roles of teachers and of pupils readily become habitual. This means that the system must not demand any role conflict or apparent changes of personality as people move from one process within it to another. All the processes it incorporates must be manageable in the same terms of personal relationship and they must be as manageable for as many personal styles as there are people. Nor should the processes call for quite different kinds of decisions to be made. A simple democratic system encouraging democratic development needs to allow for frequent, immediate local decisions to be made within a wide general understanding of the constraints of the system. The distinction I have been forced to make so frequently in this book between face values and working values has to be made unnecessary. I suggest that our touchstone for all the processes we bring into play should be the extent of possible collaboration allowed for in each, and it is from this point of view that I intend to describe the processes we envisage as contributing to the operation of a *fourfold curriculum.*

A Fourfold Curriculum

What follows is an amalgam of my own observations, my colleagues' theoretical contributions to the collaborative critique of secondary schooling which has been going on for four years now in our curriculum laboratory, and the insights of all the teachers who have collaborated with us and who keep us fully informed of the difficulties that crop up when they make innovations in their schools.

It is of course out of such revelations of difficulties, statement and restatement of aims discussed in schools and among innovators meeting in the laboratory and elsewhere, that all the work represented in this book, and our description of a fourfold curriculum has grown. Most of the theoretical review I have so far presented has been hindsight and the system I am recommending has not itself been systematically designed. Our first aim was to establish some neutral ground, a kind of protected but very open field in which fresh perceptions of familiar scenes could flourish. Our first professional concern is still to keep the field open but also to encourage teachers to test new procedures of their own which express their new insights and to go on sharing their findings with each other.

The initial demand the members of the first Goldsmiths' Pilot Course set themselves was simultaneously to unstream and to eliminate subject barriers by organizing team teaching around the exploration of a theme meant to occupy the attention of all children in a year age group and planned to last a school year. Each school worked out its own version of this approach and a small volunteer team of teachers in a number of schools were beginning to operate their schemes when our second course of teachers assembled. The process was warmly opened to observation by our new group and ourselves and this process has continued to the point where my colleague Leslie Smith has to maintain an elaborate communications network and publish a bulletin called *Ideas* to keep people in touch with each other.

I shall try to reveal honestly all the snags I have observed in schools and which have been reported to us in the following chapters. Here I want only to outline the fourfold curriculum as we at present see it—a view arrived at by attempting continually to redefine schooling as a system in the light of cumulative criticism of recent innovations.

I must warn against any attempt to view the system as a structure of four fixed pieces. What I am describing is four ways of organizing the collaborations of teachers with youngsters, each of which is meant to cope with a different group of needs. The interplay of these four organizations can vary all the time. It is this possibility that gives the system the necessary flexibility. The system overall is meant to enable the development of a much greater authenticity of relationships, which is the primary requisite for achieving democratic socialization. The system is not a set of pigeon holes into which kinds of subject matter can be sorted; any discipline may contribute to an interdisciplinary enquiry or be handled autonomously or do both. Nor does any one of the four organizations have a fixed dominance over the others. But since my description is predictive (no school has yet developed a fourfold curriculum quite in the way I am describing) the order of innovations throws most weight first on the introduction of inter-disciplinary enquiry, since that is the part missing completely from streamed, subject timetabled schools. To introduce inter-disciplinary enquiry begins a chain of changes in the organiza-tion of other procedures in the school. The end of that chain of changes will, I think, be found to be such a system as I describe.

The account I offer of the four complementary organizations is not meant to be definitive. Each is a starting point which will be amplified and qualified in the following chapters.

Setting up a fourfold curriculum is not a way of resolving quarrels between staff over allocations of resources, time and prestige. Unless the good of all parties—community, pupils and teachers—is intended and unless the curriculum is seen as a flexible system of complementary *processes*, it will merely become a new container for old, unaltered attitudes. Part of the change intended must be to take the weight off our reliance on teaching and put it more on diversity of ways of learning. With this goes the intention to organize for diversity; and coupled with that a desire to free the learners from the confusing maze of separated learning events which now composes secondary schooling so that they may find continuity in their learning.

We think of the fourfold curriculum as a range of learning situations which is open-ended with purely social constraints at one end of the continuum and confined at the other by what we take to be the necessary sequence of information and experiences which best enables a particular, limited skill to be acquired. I am not arguing for general education versus specialization or for selfdirected learning versus instruction. I am arguing for a system of collaborations which will allow us to provide *all* the necessary diversity of situations and at the same time achieve a greater authenticity of personal knowledge which can transform our purely instructional practices to allow for diversity there too. In Bruner's terms, part of what must be achieved by interdisciplinary enquiry is "activation of explora-tion" and part of what is achieved by instruction in the other studies is reassurance and confirmation of skills. Yet the other studies are not to be mere instructional devices. Nor at any point where we see ourselves clearly as instructors should we be incapable of coming up with several ways of instructing:

> The maintenance of exploration, once it has been activated, requires that the benefits from exploring alternatives exceed the risk incurred. Learning something with the aid of an instructor should be less dangerous or risky than learning on one's own . . . . There are usually various sequences that are equivalent in their ease and difficulty for learners. There is no unique sequence for all learners and the optimum in any case will depend on a variety of factors.[5]

Bruner, like Piaget, has unfortunately been much more heavily used as an authority to support even more structuring of learning events than as a guide away from class teaching. His own thinking in fact recognizes what I have called collaborative learning—he calls it reciprocity. Perhaps he should have talked of a first, rather than of a last motive:

> One last intrinsic motive that bears closely upon the will to learn. Perhaps it should be called reciprocity. For it involves a deep human need to respond to others, and to operate jointly with them towards an objective . . . you cannot have reciprocity and the demand that everybody learn the same thing or be "completely" well rounded in the same way all the time. If reciprocally operative groups are to give support to learning by stimulating each person to join his efforts to a group, then we shall need tolerance for the specialized roles that develop—the critic, the innovator, the second helper, the cautionary.[6]

Bruner here is still more individualist than I am. I feel that we are instinctually driven into collaboration and that it does more than "give support to learning." As he says in the same essay, without taking up its implications fully:

> A child in a baseball game behaves baseball; in the drugstore the same child behaves drugstore. Situations

114

have a demand value that appears to have little to do with the motives that are operative.

A child in school behaves school—where the basic motive is frustrated. Our aim with a fourfold curriculum is to allow the child and his teachers to behave in four ways *which do not conflict*, expressed as four different learning setups, clearly distinguished and yet equally valued and equally available.

Summary

1. All the purposes for which schooling is provided can be met by four complementary organizations of collaboration between teachers and pupils, each of which copes with a different set of requirements, given that the overall system enables authenticity of relationship and so of personal knowledge of the needs of the pupils. On the basis of this knowledge of needs and of developing interests and capacities, such a system would be flexible enough for appropriate decisions to be taken about each pupil's use of time in studies covered by the four types of organization described below.

2. *Interdisciplinary enquiry.* This should be genuinely interdisciplinary from the staff point of view and genuine enquiry from the pupil's point of view. Major questions or problems of concern to the youngsters should be located and explored in small collaborative groups. Teachers should act as advisers, not directors, offering the benefits of their mature commonsense as well as their specialist expertise and helping to put the youngsters in touch with other people or resources demanded by the progress of the enquiry. They should especially try to help by offering methodological advice and criticism enabling the youngsters to become more aware of the processes of hypothesis and prediction they are using. Teachers should also sensitize themselves to deeper observation of the collaborative interaction within the small groups and between groups. A small group or cluster of children

occasionally collaborating with another cluster is to be preferred to a large group, even where both groups are largely duplicating the same work. Effective collaboration without clear division of labor falls off rapidly as group size grows beyond five members.

3. *Autonomous studies.* Directed by teachers to a pattern determined by teachers, these studies will be organized to meet predicted needs, to implement decisions based on considerations other than the observed needs of the children, or to meet widely observed common needs which become apparent as common difficulties in successfully carrying out interdisciplinary enquiries. If you want many of your pupils to begin learning French and they don't make the demand, you teach it. If numbers of them are attempting to use statistical techniques in their selfdirected studies, you teach statistics to the appropriate level. Apparent failures and gaps which are not so widespread are better coped with by remedial studies. Autonomous studies may be timetabled in the conventional way but they may also be covered by crash programs or by a wide range of techniques from mass visits, lecture, or film viewing to individual programmed learning. We need not limit ourselves to timetabling the school day or week; it is quite possible to think of timetabling areas of the school year, giving over long stretches of time to intensive autonomous studies.

4. *Remedial studies.* This organization enables all teachers to act as tutors rather than as class teachers or general specialist advisers to help individual students overcome specific stumbling blocks which may be holding up their studies. Each team or focus group of teachers supervising the interdisciplinary enquiries of a year group of youngsters needs to have one member at least who watches for such individual stumbling blocks and channels the pupil to the teacher best equipped to help remedy the situation. This should be standard procedure and not in any way shameful for the student. Where any child seems to be very disaster prone, the focus group of teachers should carefully decide the priorities for remedial studies and not overload the child nor have him

so much withdrawn for remedial studies that he ceases to play a significant part in the work of his cluster. In remedial studies even more than in autonomous studies a school should develop a wide range of programs for remedial use from cumulative experience. This organization should completely replace the withdrawn fixed grouping of backward children into remedial classes.

5. *Special interest studies.* These studies (incorporating hobbies and specialization) should be organized to enable children of whatever age who enjoy a common interest, in work or a special kind of play, to get together with teachers who also share those interests and pursue them. Where no teacher shares those interests, a parent, neighbor, or one of the older students should be encouraged to act as organizer. This organization should not be a rag-bag category which covers anything left out in the other three; it should be used positively to encourage the young to seek out people who share their interests and to engage themselves deeply in learning together. It is perhaps especially important for the most highly creative children that their youth should not bar them from meeting people who can encourage and help them, so the organization should extend beyond the school into the community and enable the pupil to be released from school to pursue special interest studies as an important integral part of his schooling. If a school is unstreamed and this provision is not made the most eager children may indeed be held back.

References

1. Anthony Sampson, *Anatomy of Britain Today* (Hodder and Stoughton, 1965; Harper and Row, 1966).
2. Robert Jenkins, Superintendent of Schools San Francisco, reported in the *San Francisco Chronicle* (November 18, 1966).
3. Laurence Stenhouse, "Open Minded Teaching," in *New Society* (July 24, 1969).

4. William Sargant, "The Physiology of Faith," in *New Society* (July 17, 1969).
5. Jerome Bruner, *Toward a Theory of Instruction* (Harvard University Press, 1966; OUP, 1966).
6. See note 5 above.

CHAPTER 5

Interdisciplinary Enquiry

Since it calls for the most complex collaborations and for the least definition of tasks and immediate objectives, inter-disciplinary enquiry is the most complex of the four processes. It is neither a substitute for nor an extension of primary school project methods and it should not be handled as an instructional method, nor as a way of leading to conclusions predetermined by the teachers. No holds, no media, no questions should be barred. Once established in a school it should become a continuous process of collaborative decisions made between a focus group of teachers and clusters of pupils on what to tackle next and how to proceed. To reach this stage may well take as long as three years during which time the initiative lies mainly with the teachers. I will deal later with the problems of bringing it into the curriculum.

There are many techniques through which the enquiring mind realizes its world. All of these should be regarded as appropriate and the whole range encouraged to develop without a preference for written work of the kind now called for most frequently in school. Role playing, other kinds of simulation, invention of games, controlled experiments, experiments in observation, sensual exercises, studies in perception and inter-personal perception, modelling, all kinds of making, all of which takes place amidst continual discussion of what they are doing among the youngsters themselves, is to be aimed for. It is wise not to plan the process in the light of the type casting we normally apply to youngsters in school. Even the distinction between convergers and divergers can break down or at least come to look very different from the distinctions that appear when the children are "behaving school" when convergers produce predictable convergent behavior. Conventionally regarded, convergers allow themselves fewer ideas to play with than divergers and focus more narrowly on sequential steps of argument or procedure. Interdisciplinary enquiry, in that it allows for much deflection as a result of interaction within and between groups, might seem tough on convergers. In fact it may benefit them greatly as their tidiness in procedures will greatly enhance the efficiency of their cluster, while the cluster in turn opens them to more possibilities. There is some evidence that convergence, as encouraged by streaming and class teaching, is genuinely damaging to the convergers themselves in that they become insensitive to other people and likely to demand from everybody the kind of conformism that suits them. Liam Hudson, who presents such evidence, also found that when he approached a group with tests and changed his usual bland hectoring authoritarian signal, the divergers in the group—markedly convergent members of the class—produced very high scores on an open-ended test where such boys usually produced few ideas. The fact was everybody worked harder than usual. Convergers *do* have a divergent capacity which they normally underexploit. Interdisciplinary enquiry conducted collabora-tively in clusters, with teachers clearly signalling that their role in this situation is advice and not instruction, can encourage the exploitation of divergent ability while at the same time reducing the risk of damaging sensitivity:

... in a highly competitive and stratified school boys are saturated with convergent reasoning. They assume that this and the ability to get good examination marks are one and the same; and the more successful they are, the more perceptive about each other's powers of convergent reasoning they become. Conversely, the more successful they are, the less sensitive they are to each other's capacity to diverge.[1]

How then are we to decide what is being studied in interdisciplinary enquiry? How do we decide what topics to offer? The short answer is, we don't. Invite the young to throw up questions which they find sufficiently important to want to explore and help them to set up those explorations methodically and imaginatively. At first they will not trust the situation (and nor will you) and they will offer suggestions that seem appropriate to schooling as they know it. But as they gain confidence and faith in your backing, they will soon begin to produce in school the questions that they otherwise mull over in and among themselves.

I can best bring out the peculiar quality of the learning we can expect to be demanded by the students—characteristically adolescent learning both in content and in social style—by quoting extensively from reports by Edward Blishen[2] and Royston Lambert.[3] Blishen's evidence comes from entries to a newspaper competition on "The School I'd Like" and is vigorously but decorously expressed. Lambert's evidence is largely from diaries kept for him and for his highly expert interviewers by youngsters in boarding schools. The very far from decorous expression in these diaries is a tribute to the interviewers; one very rarely gets such frankness on paper from the young as this revelation of a sixteen-year-old boy's difficulty in coping with the sheer impersonality of the learning he's expected to do, and of how hostile the timetabled day is to him:

Now the full shag begins to hit you. O god—sorry, you correct yourself, O God—four bloody lessons in a row . . . here's Maxwell, the master. You feel surprised at the vicious intensity of your own thoughts. Forty minutes pass. You're not really working—you know you're not going to pass your A levels 'cos you just fritted away your time feeling I can't work there's no incentive. I wonder what Penny's doing now? I want a motorbike only the silly sod of a father I've got won't give it me. No he's not a silly sod really, be loyal .... O god—God—Maxwell's asked me a question. I'm going red, sweating .... Attention switches me off. Bell.[4]

It very clearly is not only children of low ability who find the curriculum of our secondary schools irrelevant, as the Newsom report suggested. The system is hostile to adolescence, which demands personal conviction and personal experience and higher standards of responsibility than adults seem to offer them:

> I ... must learn to live in your word-covered world
> And learn about your things.
> Calling a leaf green instead of looking;
> And never knowing that in your lives you had Auschwitz ...[5]

Examinations are very much resented and not merely because they contain so much that is irrelevant, but because the youngsters recognize that the time spent on them is robbing them of what they do want to learn. It isn't just that "The curriculum is designed with only one thing in mind—exams. There's no discussion, no variety" and that "It's either science or arts. If you're good at subjects like English and biology you have had it here."[6] They actively mistrust the categories in which knowledge is offered them; "Because what does exist, or has existed, is taught in our schools under the superficial names of geography or history, very little attention is paid to what might exist, and so the benefit of the acquired knowledge is never properly used."[7]

Interdisciplinary enquiry has to cope with all of this. The objectives are opportunity to work uninterrupted by bells for whole sessions, without the kind of standardization called for by examination, with freedom to exercise a personal style of learning and with no discouragement of speculation which is utterly essential to adolescence. But there is more:

The fault with a lot of schools today is that teachers are

not prepared to listen .... They don't mind discussing various topics as long as it ends up with them being able to prove a point to you and not the other way.[8]

So there is a demand for teachers' involvement, as long as they can be open minded and avoid steering enquiries back into the old categories. It is this that demands a new kind of collaboration between teachers as a focus group, not as representatives in an interdepartmental committee. Interdisciplinary enquiry is not a battlefield on which to defend the territory of your subject. It is an open field in which to demonstrate the skills you have at your command as a result of mastering the discipline of your subject.

The bitterest resentment expressed again and again is at the lack of opportunity for discussion, not of the point to point hurdling race kind that we're all familiar with, but of a more discursive, rambling kind. This means not that teachers must tolerate the fact that the young gossip more among themselves while they work, but that the teachers must bring themselves to enjoy discursive talking, without hurrying towards closures of the matters in hand or hasty categorization of the topics the young like to handle as confused groups.

What are the concerns of the young? I find them equally well expressed in this:

> All the cracking of slums is only a start,
> And even the noble "Less testing, more Art"
> Will not give the arrogant a quick change of heart.[9]

and in this:

> Stew, mash, carrots for lunch, quite disgusting, conversation flared over dying, work, the bomb, the pill, sociology, GCE and work once more.[10]

Finally and basically, the concerns shared by teachers and pupils must be authentic. The young know perfectly well what inauthenticity does to them:

> Respect for the pupil is just as important as respect for the teacher, because after a young person's opinion has been

disregarded three or four times the young person may never express an opinion again.[11]

Blishen himself summarizes concisely the kind of content we shall find the young seeking to deal with in interdisciplinary enquiries when they stop "behaving school:"

> They call for new kinds of curriculum in which they can follow up a wave of interest until it is, for the moment, spent; or in which a number of associated subjects are made to serve a single enquiry . . . . They want projects, and to be allowed to build their work out of all sorts of subject matter round central interests . . . . Again and again they asked to be introduced to philosophy, psychology, logic; to learn about current affairs, politics, modern machines, human relationships, local government, budgeting. You would think, says a boy, that such highly important concerns . . . were almost "leprous," so carefully are they avoided in most schools.[12]

The call is clearly for enquiry, not for integrated studies, and for opportunities to *do* something, to explore powers of action, as well as for verbal speculation. The young can be dispassionate and reasonable enough but they cannot be impersonal, nor can the learning they are seeking be encompassed without action. It is not merely more initiative in deciding on topics to study in school that interdisciplinary enquiry should allow for. The way into adult life for the adolescent is through ruminative speculation, shared with a few of his fellows, leading to visions of possible courses of action. Frustrate the action and you frustrate the true intellectual developments for which the adolescent is ready and which are likely to wither in the bud if the season of readiness is missed.

Jean Piaget, in the concluding ten pages of his essay on *The Mental Development of the Child*, gives a perfectly lucid picture of what all adolescents must do if they are to go forward from childhood, the balance of speculation and action that must be achieved, the necessity of both speculation and action:

> By comparison with a child, an adolescent is an individual

who constructs systems and theories .... what is striking
in the adolescent is his interest in theoretical problems not
related to everyday realities .... The majority talk about
only a small part of their personal creations and confine
themselves to ruminating about them intimately and in
secret. But all of them have systems and theories that
transform the world in one way or another ....
Equilibrium is attained when the adolescent understands
that the proper function of reflection is not to contradict
but to predict and interpret experience.[13]

Here we find the reason for the discursive kind of discussion
adolescents value most and for their seemingly untidy attempt
to "yoke heterogeneous ideas violently together" as Johnson
accused Donne of doing (perhaps a good reason for Donne's
everlasting appeal to the young and all divergers). For anything
to have meaning for the young it must be relevant to a trial
system that is a "transformation of the world." All becomes
grist to that mill and it matters not at all what content is
demanded by youngsters in the process of interdisciplinary
enquiry, so long as it transcends limits of obsessional triviality.
Here we can trust the collaborative setup for two reasons; first
it allows the young to work in the coteries they themselves
prefer; but second, the dialogue which is always present and the
shared perception of values can deflect any individual from
trivialities into deeper concerns; and teachers of course can play
a part in this, not by dismissing any topic or opinion as
irrelevant but through collaboration.

And this will work especially well where collaboration is
encouraged to get something done about the state of the world,
or some part of it at least. Turning to Piaget again for guidance,
it is possible to distinguish between the kind of project learning
which is needed before puberty and the kind of project which
can really serve as a focal expression of the quite different needs
of adolescents:

The young child unwittingly models the world on his own
image but nonetheless feels inferior to adults and the older
children whom he imitates. He thus fashions a kind of

separate world at a level below the world of his elders. The adolescent on the other hand . . . sees himself as equal to his elders, yet different from them, different because of the new life stirring within him. He wants to surpass and astound them by transforming the world . . . . The phenomenon is the same whether it has to do with the misunderstood and anxious youngster convinced of failure who questions the value of life itself or with the active youngster convinced of his own genius . . . . The adolescent in all modesty attributes to himself an essential role in the salvation of humanity and organizes his life plan accordingly.[14]

This idealism (which is a universal phenomenon of youth, and which shows up most tragically strongly where it appears as disillusion, cynicism or despair in the young gangster who has read only too accurately the signals that society wants no part of his powers, but sees power as belonging only to others, people not like him) does not need to merge in absolute parity with adults as regards political control of society. It is only when the drive is frustrated that the young make unreasonable demands and start chewing over more than they can bite off. It can be very well satisfied by conservation projects (and we have a desperate need for thousands of such projects to be carried out) and in inventive rather than routine contribution of evident usefulness to other individuals or society at large. Of course their inventiveness will often quarrel with our routine measures for dealing with some problems and they will as often as not be right. Teachers at least must be open minded about such possibilities, and may need to become propagandists to some extent for their pupils. But since, as a despairing American professor was heard to remark, "There's still some life left around in the interstices of the bureaucracy," there is still plenty of room for action in areas where there is no quarrel for the right to act.

Often such projects, given that they demand a complex enough variety of action, can contain everything that we aim for in interdisciplinary enquiry. They can arise in a phase of enquiry and once under way become routine and so be reclassified as personal interest studies, leaving time free again to undertake another enquiry, perhaps of a different kind. One of Lambert's subjects, a boy at a public school which had undertaken a social service scheme to preserve the flora and restock the fauna of neighboring meadows by lowering the water level, reveals the extent of learning and personal satisfaction he gets from it:

Funny, isn't it . . . . I hated science—dropped every subject fast. I hated manual—what little we did of it. They put me on the water meadow scheme against my will—what, *me* splashing around in that slime? Well, you live and learn. I'm out there now regularly in waders. I love the water, the mud oozing through my fingers, the sense of working with nature. I love watching the trout grow in the stew ponds, studying the force and direction of currents and the effect they will have on drainage and the growth of river plants and insect life. This scheme has opened a new world, made me feel more organic.[15]

Lamentably few schools are favored enough to have water meadows handy, but projects demanding wide study along with inventiveness do not have to be of that kind. The pupils of Wanstead High School who have now been given funds to set up a specialist workshop for the purpose learned quite as much tackling the problem of designing custom built furniture, transport and various aids for cripples, as well as benefiting from the personal contact with their clients. And the boys in a school in Jersey who decided to explore the problem of designing toys for toddlers gave themselves sophisticated problems of observing the development of muscular coordination involved in manipulating toys (and consequently very tough problems of design) as well as finding it necessary to look carefully into the meaning of play for the children. Such work is useful and positive; it has a product and the field of study is genuinely interdisciplinary. (It was undertaken, I am assured, by "very ordinary" boys.)

Only the third of these projects I have cited was undertaken under the umbrella of interdisciplinary enquiry. The benefit of incorporating such practical approaches into the curriculum fully instead of as out-of-school activities, is that far more of the implications can, if they prove interesting enough, be taken up and that there is a focus group of teachers waiting and ready to help in just that way. This can be fed back into decisions about the rest of the youngsters' schooling, remedies can be applied, a different pattern of autonomous studies prescribed as quite new specialist interests appear, and this new insight into the youngsters' capacities can help us shape the whole of their schooling into a more appropriate pattern.

The starting point for a fresh phase of interdisciplinary enquiry in a school where it is practised, or to introduce it into the curriculum of a school for the first time, does not have to be a topic. There are at least three ways of entry into the process. Which one is most appropriate for any given school depends on the present state of relationships (which affects the frankness with which youngsters will express deep concern rather than trivial but safe interests to their teachers), the personal skill, specialist expertise and confidence of the focus group of staff who are to supervise the work, and the school's environment as a possible field for experiment. In all cases there are some common preparatory measures that have to be taken—decisions affecting the organization of the school. But if the process is to be genuinely one of enquiry, the actual conduct of the enquiry should not be perfectly predictable.

The first decision to be made is who shall teach and what children shall be included. Here two factors are of overwhelming importance—the willingness and the readiness of staff and youngsters to experiment. These matter much more than the specialist expertise of the teachers or the presumed academic abilities of the students. The aim after all is to help the young achieve some overall complex improvement in their learning behavior by activating exploration. It is important that the system of masking failures that comes into play in learning-event situations should break down here and that we locate instead the kinds of positive contribution the young make to their clusters, the style of work each prefers, and help them build on that. There isn't as in class teaching a starting point of what the child knows of the subject, nor a goal of so many more items of knowledge to be grasped. The increased stock or transformed condition of information acquired in the process of enquiry is a secondary consideration. It should be observed of course but the process is designed to enable us to observe something more important which cannot be seen in any other situation—each individual's own personal style of seeking to know. If we measure anything it is each youngster's improvement of his own performance. It is like measuring a child's physical growth against a wall. He isn't expected to grow until he is level with the top of the wall, nor is there a starting line on the wall below which we don't bother to measure him. We just scratch a mark where his head reaches from time to time so that he can see how much he has grown.

Absolute measures of success in terms of information handled, which are appropriate in some autonomous studies and in remedial work, are not relevant to the process of interdisciplinary enquiry. There is really no line that can be drawn between exploring ourselves and exploring the world. We know ourselves in knowing what we do, in the picture we build of our strengths. In exploration we need to know our own ability to go on; we need an awareness of the techniques that suit us best and this is what we should be helping children to discover in the course of their enquiries. And this is the pivot of the interplay between interdisciplinary enquiry and other processes in the curriculum. Strengths and interests discovered here and which prove persistent become the basis on which we make our decisions about time to be spent in more highly structured studies. As Leslie Smith puts it:

> By basing educational experiences around the detected strong points, the school will be seen by the pupil to be aware of at least one of his needs . . . the specially devised experiences can be devised to *work from the relative strength* and so to enhance the possibility that other behavioral characteristics may be encouraged to develop within the pupil. Finally the school can demonstrate that it places emphasis on the pupil's relatively strong features

and respects them for what they are; and herein are the ingredients of encouragement which can be made available to all pupils.[16]

There is no need at all specially to devise groupings of the children. The best initial clusters (which may be left naturally to recluster where deflection comes into play as the actual developments of work direct) are clusters of children who happen to be friends already. The same is true of the staff group. They should at least be compatible; they should be volunteers; they should not be a committee, approaching each other formally.

This need to avoid formality positively within the focus group sets an upper limit on its size (I think it unwise to have more than five members) and this in turn sets an upper limit on the tribe of children attached to a particular focus group, of say 150. That may sound a frightful number; in fact it is quite manageable if the teachers themselves are enjoying authentic relationships with each other and are not therefore compulsively selfcontrolling and, as a result, compulsive meddlers in the children's work. Whatever setup is envisaged the youngsters must, once agreements have been made about a phase of work, be allowed and encouraged to get on with it and to approach the teachers when they need them, not to expect the teachers to approach them. This is a sensitive matter of course and teachers will decide for themselves when to intrude. Intrusion isn't forbidden and it's often needed. As authenticity of personal knowledge improves, the situation sorts itself out and you get used to keeping a watchful eye ever open for about one child in ten, meaning that five teachers have fifteen problems on their hands.

It is as well for the focus group to contain volatile as well as steady elements and it helps if all the members are as interested in media as they are in subject disciplines. There needs to be somebody with an interest in three-dimensional structures (it need not actually be a skilled crafts teacher, a chemist may well have better structural sense than an unenterprising woodwork expert), somebody with a good graphic sense (an amateur photographer or a modern geographer may well have a better eye and eikonic sense of diagram than an art teacher), and somebody who is personally imaginative and speculative, likely to defend the right of youngsters to explore even the oddest ideas. Since the focus group is formed in this way, it needs to get the support of other members of the staff who will act as discipline consultants and have some time allowed for advising youngsters on subject matter that lies beyond the scope of the focus group itself. Knowing the times these people are available the focus group can channel students to them or seek advice themselves. If there is sufficient demand, the focus group can also decide at any time to suspend the enquiries of a number of clusters and call in an expert from the staff or from outside to deal with a specific topic a number of students have veered into, like the neighboring baker at one school, who enormously enjoys being called on for culinary hints and also for first hand geography gathered in the course of thirty years travelling as ship's cook. The focus group can also decide to give common instruction themselves, especially in the exploitation of under-exploited media. For example the camera is a much better tool of observation for many purposes than pencil and notebook, so the focus group may decide to give everybody a crash course in photography or in collage or in diagrammatic representation of information.

The initial decisions made should be of a kind which will allow rapid, effective decisions to be carried out in the course of enquiry. The focus group should be friendly; time given to consultants should coincide with the times scheduled for enquiry; enough time should be allowed for the youngsters to work at their own pace and rhythm (at least three whole sessions of a ten session week, with uninterrupted mornings or afternoons); space allotted should be flexible without too much fixed furniture. It is best to allot contiguous spaces. If that cannot be done, it doesn't much matter if you are prepared to find that small nomadic groups do a good deal of travelling around the school. Such a school is much pleasanter and less panicky than one in which traffic jams develop when everybody has to change rooms at the same time. You also have to decide how far you are prepared to allow clusters to pursue their enquiries outside school, in streets, workshops, factories, libraries or museums, and finally you must make provision for storing incompleted work and exhibiting completed projects. This last point is particularly important. Displaying completed projects contributes so much to the deflection and general creative ferment as well as to the selfesteem of the students who are continually demonstrating their achievements by publishing them. This problem of redesigning schools so that they become workshops/museums/artshows, has to be referred to the architects but it is at least necessary to be aware before you begin a change of process that exercise books which can be stored in desks are used very little by adolescents working collaboratively. Paper, where it is used, will be in large sheets that can be hung up like a newspaper on the wall and allow for complex mosaic format. The exercise book enforces linearity and by cutting down the possibilities of cross reference cuts back the work done to far too naive a level. Somehow there must be opportunities to exhibit work and not to have it knocked about. All the young people I have observed working in this way take far more pride in their work than we ever take in notebooks. Indeed I always come away wishing I could have brought something away with me to keep, and work which escapes all categorization—is it art, sociology or biology?—seen hanging on a classroom wall two years ago, remains as clear in my memory as Dürer's rhinoceros—is it art or zoology?

Decisions interlock of course. Most of our schools are far too small anyway, having been designed as filing cabinets for a fixed volume of people rather than as workshops. In such schools, the first expedient is to decide to depopulate the school by using it more as a base camp from which to explore the world and less as a child concentration camp. The kind of overtidiness which militates against worthwhile work develops only where people are constantly worried and fretful at overcrowding. Interdisciplinary enquiry and special interest studies will both be outgoing, while most of the remedial and autonomous studies will be school confined.

So much for guidelines to decisions about staffing, time and space. The other initial decision to be made by a school introducing enquiry into its curriculum for the first time has to be what age group of children to begin with. Here the readiness of the youngsters and staff and the current organization of the school become important. If the school is in any case unstreamed and has used team teaching with some integration of subjects, a start could easily be made with any year group. The children will already be used to their right to produce diverse responses in the classroom. In a streamed school where the decision will involve abandoning streaming, it will be best to start with the first year intake divided into two randomly assembled tribes with two focus groups if the school has more than five entry forms. These youngsters, coming from primary schools where the day has been fairly flexible, will not have to unlearn habits of subject timetabling. The other group in most streamed British schools which will be ready for enquiry will be the fourth and fifth year students who have written off their schooling anyway. The danger is that they will suspect that this method is just another attempt to win them over. Still, once begun the process recommends itself. It is worth undertaking for the youngsters' own sake but the staff will learn less from the experience of initiating enquiry with the tail enders of streaming than from initiating it with a mixed-up unknown population.

Whichever age group is first included the pioneer corps of teachers making up the first focus group need support from the head and from colleagues, and they will definitely need to be given time set aside for nothing but discussion and making arrangements, say half a morning a week when they can talk and plan and telephone. In the long run, once they are used to the process they will be able to make their own time for this, but in the early days they will be under stress, worrying how far they should try to control everything, and they will not have built up enough personal contacts to allow the children to go out often to work with known people in the community. They will be using a lot of energy in making frequent on-the-spot decisions of an unfamiliar kind and in controlling traffic which will later become selfregulating, as will the traffic of individuals through the four processes of the fourfold curriculum when enquiry has become a familiar enough process for it to modify other processes.

How I expect those modifications to come about and what effect I expect them to have on the whole problem of educational assessment I shall explain later in a short section on each of the processes. I am giving most of my attention and space to interdisciplinary enquiry because this is the least familiar process and the most likely to be misunderstood.

I said earlier that I see three distinct ways into the process of enquiry. In fact there are as many modes as there are personal learning styles and recognized disciplines of study, and the purpose of setting up systematic situations for interdisciplinary enquiry in schools is to allow for the fruition of all of these. So in a reformed curriculum there should no longer be problems of finding ways in, but rather problems of expansion and carrying on, and these should be solved by greater authenticity of relationships, greater readiness to collaborate. The hunger of youngsters for novelties of vision which support their inwardly generated attempt to transform the world should also solve the problem of keeping the curriculum up to date, since they will provoke their teachers to be more alert to displacements of theories in all fields. What I have to say here about ways of starting should not be read as an attempt to fix modes of enquiry in distinct categories. All I am doing is suggesting three strategies for approaching the same problem of how to get a whole tribe of youngsters to divide themselves into small clusters and produce schemes of study which seem to them and their teachers worth pursuing energetically.

"Schemes of study" sounds very much like "book learning" and the initial reaction of most children conditioned by our kind of schooling will indeed be to ask the teachers what books they should turn to, as if they had been asked the question "What do you want to find out about?" It should be made clear to them at the start that this kind of enquiry is meant to cover "finding out" at first hand by experiment as well as "finding out about" by using books, films and so on for reference and that it is also acceptable for them to make discoveries through intensively practical activity and present what they have made as the product of their learning rather than a description of it.

So the three ways in—which could of course be combined—are:

1. Offer a topic or theme broad enough to lend itself to a rich variety of interpretations like "Growing Up," "Islands," "Violence," "Power" or something more specific still but equally broad like "Living in a Technological Society." Predict likely responses and prepare for them as well as possible with resource material and suggestions for experiments, and begin by giving a vigorous presentation of stimuli with talks, films, visits and so on. After that get clusters to offer schemes of study.
2. Plan more carefully with cores of common experience which guarantee diverse experience to each youngster and are likely to generate very diverse approaches.
3. Plan a complex practical project of conservation, or in some other way socially useful, which is going to throw up theoretical and practical problems covering many disciplines, with the aim of encouraging a follow-up in depth of the problems that fire the youngsters' imaginations.

The first approach is closest to current common practice and may be the easiest for many teachers to achieve at the first go. If it is adopted some care is needed to provoke unconventional responses, as otherwise many children scuttle for safety into well-worn routines of note making with very little first-hand quality. Discovery always involves taking risks and if a whole cluster is playing safe the teachers may need to step in with firm suggestions for alternative experimental modes of learning with the intent of taking discussion to deeper, more fundamental levels. Given this intervention, youngsters who begin by playing safe can produce very remarkable work.

A case that comes to mind is of the thirteen-year-old girl who reinvented for herself the concept of alienation (which of course she had never heard of) as "grey slavery." Her route to this discovery is not untypical of what happens in thematic interdisciplinary enquiry, not untypical even in the maturity of her thinking, but interesting in the insight it gave her teachers into her personal style and the part played in her life by visual thinking, which we still consistently underrate in our schools. She began with the theme "The Sea" in common with her year group and worked first with a somewhat literary coterie, reading stories and poems and writing their own with illustrations. She was moved by the discovery she made of *The Ancient Mariner*. Her imaginative work was of high quality; mostly it represented sorrow, loneliness and obsession with death, a theme which is terribly important to all adolescents, but taboo in our society and hardly ever allowed to surface in schools. She wrote herself out, and evidently puzzled herself, since her next move was a retreat into the tidy occupation of keeping a log for a boat, getting information from people as well as from books and integrating it as a diary. She learned a good deal about small boats by the way. This became boring and she was restive in her cluster too, wanting to work more on her own. At this point she was deflected as so often happens in this setup; a youngster wanders, waiting for a worthwhile idea, a very important process indeed as all creative workers know. The best ideas form themselves somehow and emerge at a right moment which is signalled by a sudden fresh perception of something familiar or come upon randomly. Others were working on the slave trade, clued initially by a copy of the *Observer* color supplement which contained, among other pictures, a diagram of the layout of the slave cargo in a French slave ship.

This diagram became a coordinator for her. She first wrote a short history of the slave trade and then sought advice on techniques of surveying, built a questionnaire to detect color prejudice, interviewed many girls in her school, parents and neighbors and classified responses with rudimentary attempts to look for influence of background. She presented a summary of her findings in various diagrams, the concluding one being the slave ship itself with people who have warm feelings to people, including black people, as black figures, and people with hostile feelings as empty white figures. But the bulk of space is taken up by grey figures who are not, as the girl demonstrated in conversation about her work, just "don't knows," but people who seem unable to commit themselves to feeling anything at all about racial problems.

Her work of course is not conclusive and she was well aware of this. But working in this way had enabled her without realizing it to withdraw from her cluster, contribute something to the work of a group, and yet in her withdrawal enjoy serious discussion with a great many people on an issue she found worrying and important. I venture to think that this kind of tentative approach into social values is worth far more than any kind of provoked discussion can ever be. Quite incidentally she got a sound start in thinking of problems of sociological methods which hardly ever arises in taught sociology, even with youngsters three or five years older than this girl was.

The second way in, which can allow us to dispense with a theme or topic altogether, offers a common experience to all the youngsters and then leaves them free to make their plans for their continuing studies. This core can be one initial experience or a series of experiences. The core may be a conservation or social service project, or a practical redesign and restructuring of the school itself as an area for work and play. I have taken the term "core" from American core curriculum experiments but am expressing a quite opposite intention. What I mean by it is devised experience of the kind already much used by teachers within the classroom to stimulate new ideas. The public model of such events is the "happening," which is beginning to displace the play in theatres, an experience devised to unsettle and disorientate an audience so that they can react freshly to life. Teachers of English and of art, and heuristic teachers of science are all familiar with its techniques, which they are likely to refer to as ways of stimulating the imagination.

Less well known but equally significant are the techniques deliberately used in industry and scientific research to open up the minds of members of a collaborative team to each other and to the possibilities that lie beyond the reach of any of the individuals. The kinds of exercise Edward de Bono has designed for individuals[1][7] can also be devised both to help a group work more productively, as in Gordon's systems of synectics,[18] and to enable a group to share an experience of collective ferment which serves as the beginning for quite independent individual courses of action. This is at present the least well charted area of our knowledge of group dynamics, simply because our ways of organizing research and industry in the past have ignored collaboration on a large scale. Modes of collaboration are now becoming crucially important as the extent of collaboration called for, collaboration in invention by the demands of the space program most of all, increases vastly.

I don't think it possible at this stage to theorize adequately about what happens as the result of a "happening" but I do strongly favor experiments within schools. I have seen children come away from a newspaper event which simply involved having them all play (with evident enthusiastic regression to infancy) together in a school hall with hundreds of newspapers, building tents, making snow storms, doing everything that you can think of to do with paper, and outvying each other in thinking of something new to do, trying new ideas apparently quite unrelated to the event. They showed a determination to invent, an interest in materials—"Could we build a newspaper house? A newspaper town? How could we make paper stronger?"—which made interviews with clusters about their choice of studies very much more productive than an unprepared situation would have allowed for. But such an approach can only be handled by very gifted, confident teachers.

Still if you want to avoid being tied down initially by the restrictions of a theme, you can undertake a project and encourage the exploration of interesting questions that crop up and resolutions of matters that turn out to be difficult to decide. If interdisciplinary enquiry time is devoted to an open-ended project such as straight forwardly experimental work on materials in a workshop, or experiments in perception, set up with no other product in mind than to raise questions worth exploration, you are still using the second way in.

The third approach comes nearer to American core curriculum methods in that a central progressive project designed to have a finite product is used as the stimulus to discover areas worth exploring, whether or not they remain directly related to the core project. It may turn out to be the most profitable approach in the later years of secondary schooling when the youngsters' concern about their future working role is already pressing them into some sort of specialization, and when they have already developed sufficiently as specialists to be able to offer some of the subject expertise (which in the earlier years comes only from the teachers) to interdisciplinary enquiry.

The model I have been constructing for this approach, in very close collaboration with Professor John Lindbeck of Michigan and Sam Mauger, with insights added by Leslie Smith from his work on the problems of restructuring school leaving examinations, developed directly from Lindbeck's work on core curriculum in an underprivileged American high school. His core demanded that students simultaneously established by field-work enquiry in local industry the way in which specialist functions interlock and simulated the whole process by designing a workshop, setting it up and designing, making, packaging and marketing a product. Teaching of mathematics, science, economics and sociology was arranged to coincide with the phases of the simulated but very realistic production process, and the teaching of course had to face competition from what the youngsters were learning in their field work.

The simulation was not of course exact. Simulations always have an order imposed on them of events which are in fact simultaneously undertaken in real life. In this case, since it was intended that the youngsters, although they all specialized, should also all see the whole of everything that happens, the events were ordered in nine phases so that the core experience had a strict linearity.

The problem of adapting this for us in a fourfold curriculum happens to be the problem which arises anyway of maintaining some meaningful relationship between autonomous studies which respect linearity and interdisciplinary enquiry which does not. My interest in the program I am outlining therefore is in the theoretical model and I am not offering it as a realistic program for any school to put into effect. It is an attempt to see how far strict programming and open-field explorations can operate together without conflict.

Living in a Technological Society

The program is to be set up for two years—say fourth and fifth—though it could equally well cover two years of sixth form work.

The limits of interdisciplinary enquiry are set by the theme which is in fact very broad. We are allowed to question all the values of such a society. All modes of enquiry are allowed so that although industrial crafts work and design are dealt with in the simulation core as is industrial and sociological field work, other crafts and other field work may be undertaken in enquiry time.

Both enquiry and autonomous studies (except foreign languages) are related to the core. If this core is not appropriate to any number of students, another core should be planned, such as a conservation project which raises similar problems of decision making, so that its relationship to antonomous studies would be the same. Autonomous studies can then be recategorized in the nine groups shown in Table 1, to cover the fields indicated. Each calls for some integration of subjects. Not all subjects are covered in such an integration and these would be displaced to courses offered in personal interest studies time, which in a fourfold curriculum becomes the main area for specialization anyway, rather than autonomous studies which is meant to cover common basic skills instead. The two common and often conflicting demands made on subject teaching are thus split into two processes. In autonomous studies you offer what everybody needs of the subject discipline and the personal interest groups are the keen students of your subject.

The major areas of possible enquiry are also marked out in nine groups so that if students and teachers wish to relate to examinable studies they may, and the system could then cope with Mode 3 CSE examinations based on all the work done or even with reformed O and A level syllabuses.

Planned in this way, learning both in the core and in interdisciplinary enquiry takes place in collaborative clusters; in the core, the clusters also collaborate with each other and are party to all decisions that have to be made to fulfil the project, while accepting responsibility for any specialist role they play. The enquiries springing up from experience provoked by the core project add up only in an exhibition or publication of work, which explores the values of a technological society and raises questions of human scale. The balance of time given by each individual to the four processes is largely determined by the specialization allowed for in personal interest studies and by the need for time given to specific remedial exercises. New basic skills are taught and old ones extended in autonomous studies grouped in a new way, not as conventional subjects. What goes into the core is listed in Table 2, where the steps are serial. No linearity need however be observed in the areas listed as autonomous or interdisciplinary in Table 1, where the number given to each group is meant only to indicate a relationship that could be made to a phase of the linear core.

Table 1

This is a guide to the following tables which list the content of each step of the core process, the content of each of the autonomous study courses to be set up and the area of experience covered by each field of interdisciplinary enquiry. Each horizontal group in this table indicates a possible relationship of all three processes but only the core process is necessarily vertically linear. Some relationships are contrasts.

ENQUIRY	CORE	AUTONOMOUS STUDY
E1 Criteria	C1 Research	A1 Inventive exercises
E2 Graphics	C2 Production tooling	A2 Prediction
E3 Environment	C3 Production control	A3 Organization studies
E4 Leisure	C4 Quality control	A4 Measurements

E5	Selfknowledge	C5	Personnel management	A5	Microsocieties
E6	Free arts	C6	Manufacture	A6	Macrosociety
E7	Exploitation	C7	Marketing	A7	Exchange systems
E8	Human future	C8	Review: social dimensions	A8	Planning
E9	Social anthropology	C9	Review: historical dimensions	A9	Sample history

Table 2 INDUSTRIAL PROCESS AS CORE

The core is a simulation of modern industrial process in which all students share the thinking and decision making of each phase. The aim is to design, make and market a product, checking by field work in a variety of industries. The phasing of the simulation is artificial, since it avoids division of labor. Most of the processes listed as stages here are in fact undertaken simultaneously by separate groups of specialists in industry.

C1 Research. Decide what to make; experiment and research into materials; models and mock ups; design sketches.
C2 Production tooling. Design, drawing and making of tools needed to make the product.
C3 Production control. Decide layout of workshops, system of transferring materials, maintenance of equipment and work schedules.
C4 Quality control. Decide on standards to be achieved (with reference to British or international standards); determine general problems of specification and measurement; master statistics and practice of sampling techniques and apply them.
C5 Personnel management. Decide who does what; take up problems arising from modern methods of job description; selection, supervision and training of personnel; costing to include labor and bargaining.
C6 Manufacture. Look into the current variety of ways of

cutting, forming, fastening and finishing materials; make the product.

C7 Marketing. Packaging, distributing, servicing, market research, advertising, selling.

C8 Review all information gathered bearing on the social dimensions of industry. What are its present social effects? What effect on people's lives are present industrial changes having?

C9 Review all information gathered bearing on the historical dimension of industry. Which of our habits and attitudes seem to have been determined by industrialization?

Table 3 AUTONOMOUS STUDY COURSES

A1 Inventive exercises. Systematic study of techniques used for generating new ideas and improving divergent thinking—brainstorming, lateral thinking, synectics, strategic questioning (as in the game of Twenty Questions), role playing and other kinds of simulation.

A2 Prediction. Mathematics of probability; trend watching; statistics; uses of games theory.

A3 Organization studies. Business management; traffic systems of all kinds; movement analysis; flow charts; programming computers.

A4 Measurements. Problems of accuracy and approximation in mathematics and physics.

A5 Microsocieties. Interactions in small groups; personal problems of collaboration; group dynamics.

A6 Macrosociety. Social institutions as control systems.

A7 Exchange systems. Economics, with special reference to the effects of new communications technology and data storage systems.

A8 Planning. Current problems of urban national and international planning (with a strong local emphasis and action if possible in the form of setting up a conservation project which would be an alternative core study).

A9 Sample history. Exploration of the history of a specific social institution such as law. (What changes have there been in the last fifty years? Have they in any way changed the role of law?)

Table 4   FIELDS OF INTERDISCIPLINARY ENQUIRY

E1 Criteria. Exploration of the diversity of criteria used in various modes of enquiry; methodological review of personal learning.

E2 Graphics. The role played by visual thinking and by all forms of graphic representation from maps to pictures and films.

E3 Environment. Experiments in space orientation and designing a personal environment for work or relaxation.

E4 Leisure. Not reviewed as a subject, but completely free time given in school.

E5 Selfknowledge. Experiments in interpersonal perception; problems of selfassessment and selfdirection.

E6 Free art. Activities.

E7 Exploitation. Studies of the whole range of means by which man exploits the physical resources of the universe.

E8 Human future. Major problems facing the species, of predicting the human future and sharing decisions about alternative courses of action.

E9 Social anthropology. All aspects of the effects of techniques of production on social institutions.

Summary

1. Making and testing hypotheses of a world transforming scope is essential to adolescence, so a need to integrate into a personal view all that is learned becomes urgent, and this is naturally fulfilled in a highly speculative kind of dialogue, both internal and with others (especially other adolescents) and in social and practical experimentation.

2. This behavior is quite different from the information handling conducted by younger children. The world picturing now has another purpose, which includes finding a

foothold in actual adult achievement. The ideals of adolescents call for opportunities of practical attempt.

3. Neither the kind of project work which satisfies primary school children, nor integrated studies originating elsewhere than in the youngsters own personal concerns, can be used as a model for interdisciplinary enquiry.

4. Neither class groupings nor individual work schedules would fulfil the characteristic adolescent need for very tentative discussions. The basic grouping must therefore be collaborative clusters of youngsters. The assistance such clusters need can best be offered by small focus groups of teachers.

5. There should ideally be no restrictions of subject matter or of modes of discovery, problem solving, experiment or study used in interdisciplinary enquiry. It should not be confined by fashionable preferences in academic method. All media should be used and entirely practical work be welcomed.

6. When first introduced into a school, the process needs to be limited by clear guidelines. Three possible ways of beginning are with:

   i. schemes of collaborative study undertaken in clusters coordinated by an overall theme or topic offered for free interpretation and exploration

   ii. common experience of experimental work with materials, or drama or another expressive art used as a springboard to discovery of problems for clusters to explore further

   iii. setting up a long-term project with known productive objectives as a core activity encouraging clusters to take up for deeper exploration interesting side issues that crop up in discussion and decision-making sessions related to the project.

7. It is possible to combine all these approaches. There are others as yet unpredictable.

References

1. Liam Hudson, *Frames of Mind* (Methuen, 1968).
2. Edward Blisben, *The School That I'd Like* (Penguin, 1969).

3. Royston Lambert, *The Hothouse Society* (Weidenfeld and Nicolson, 1969).
4. See note 3 above.
5. See note 2 above.
6. See note 3 above.
7. See note 2 above.
8. See note 2 above.
9. See note 2 above.
10. See note 3 above.
11. See note 2 above.
12. See note 2 above.
13. Jean Piaget, Six Psychological Studies (LUP, 1968; Random House, 1968).
14. See note 13 above.
15. See note 3 above.
16. L. A. Smith, in *The Raising of the School Leaving Age*, Pilot Course Report (Goldsmiths' College, 1966).
17. E. de Bono, *The Use of Lateral Thinking* (Cape, 1967; Basic Books, 1968).
18. W. J. Gordon, *Synectics* (Harper and Row, 1961).

CHAPTER 6

Proper Studies

"Oh we do some proper studying as well," says the pupil in a pioneering school under the inquisition of a visiting teacher—youngsters are very accommodating.

The school in which I overheard this remark was one of the first to introduce interdisciplinary enquiry into its curriculum and has arrived at the stage of using all the modes I have described of beginning a new phase of study. It has also instituted a personal tutor system and got rid of the last vestiges of streaming. But there remains a clear contrast between the freedom of enquiry and the restrictive formality of autonomous studies which retain the old subject matter groupings, patterned on the requirements of school leaving examinations. The redistribution of processes hitherto all bundled inefficiently together in class teaching is still incomplete.

Interdisciplinary enquiry is *not* an alternative to instruction. It does what no system of instruction can aim to do; it lets the learner explore his own system building, his own development, in ways specifically appropriate to adolescents. It may well turn out to be an effective educational medium for other age groups too but for adolescents it is a basic necessity to have the opportunity to work in a collaborative and speculative way.

147

This opportunity has *not* been provided in our secondary schools, so we have to demand as a matter of urgency that it is added to the curriculum. It does not displace instruction in any way. It may of course achieve some of the objectives which instructors have claimed as their aims—all the character building and development of intelligence which I feel are in any case products of collaborations and more likely to be damaged than enhanced by any conceivable system of instruction.

No longer having to make long-term predictions and Falstaffian claims for the effects of instruction, we can re-examine its role in the school as a measure to achieve short-term results of specific learning. Approached from this angle, class teaching of subjects looks even odder than it did when I came at it intending to describe it as a social system, for the plain fact is that effective instruction is always individual instruction. Even programmed instruction via the machine interface has to be individuated. So the introduction of interdisciplinary enquiry will not put all right. It does away with the need for a quite separate system of pastoral care because it will improve teachers' authenticity of knowledge of their students. This improved authenticity also gives us a new basis for providing remedial instruction. But it has no direct effect on efficiency of instruction, and improvement there calls for quite other reforms.

The chief indirect effect will be to make pupils much more effectively critical of any poor instruction they may be offered and more ready to seek effective instruction. At best their successful experience of the learning they direct for themselves in interdisciplinary enquiries will enable them to take John Cage's advice:

Whenever anyone speaks informatively with precision about how something should be done, listen if you can with great interest, knowing his talk is descriptive of a single line in a sphere of illuminating potential activity, that each one of his measurements exists in a field that is wide open for exploration.[1]

Another indirect effect comes from the fact that intrusion of a new process is bound to make the teachers too more critical of what they are doing when they see themselves as instructing rather than as advising. It is not possible to opt for only one of these roles; the young expect us to play both, to be able to differentiate between them. Although in the early stages of change there may be some distribution of these roles between teachers, and the chief tool of instruction may still be class teaching, in the long run all teachers will need to be using a greater variety of techniques and responding much more finely to individual needs.

The fineness of this response to the pupils' needs depends entirely of course on the clarity—and the charity—of our view of each youngster. This is why the total system has to encourage authenticity of relationships and why timetabling has to be loosened up to the point where all schedules of work are designed as short-term agreements made between teachers and small groups or individual pupils. Simply to alternate between times given over to open enquiry and times given to class teaching planned on the old long-term syllabus model will not do. Class and subject timetabling imposes a strictly periodic rhythm of bouts of instruction decided upon without reference to the real perceived needs of any pupil. To compose a timetable for the fourfold curriculum distributing fixed quantities of time to cover the four processes would also impose an arbitrary rhythm. Begin with enquiry, detect needs there for instruction, provide the instruction through three other channels and you will find that each pupil has his own personal timetable. Its shape will largely be determined by the availability of instruction, but there will be no grand symphonic score in which everybody chips in a note on cue. This is not a total repudiation of structure. The chief fault of most of the instruction now offered in schools is that it is insufficiently structured and inappropriately structured because we insist on imposing a long-term pattern on events which need to be looked at separately. In effect we cut out the feedback (an exact knowledge of what each individual pupil is making of the instructions given) which should determine the next step we choose to take. In well-structured instruction steps are short but need not inanely avoid complexity. Literally putting one foot before the other is a complex process, not the simple "A leads to B" of dreary mechanical programmed learning.

The fourfold curriculum is meant to allow a better fulfilment of short-term objectives because it does *not* make instruction responsible for long-term development. It offers a system of four processes in interplay which can be rebalanced continually to provide the best answer possible to the needs of each individual. The pattern for each is not predetermined as a path occupying fixed sectors at fixed times. To borrow from John Cage again:

> Aperiodic rhythm admits of periodic rhythm. It doesn't work the other way around; that's why it has to be aperiodic.[2]

The fourfold curriculum is not an architectural device, a series of modules that can be locked together in various ways to produce apparently "personalized" homes. Education as a process is organic and it is collaborative. Freedom of all parties to make short-term agreements is at the heart of it and it is putting the system in gear for such agreements that matters most. All that I have to say later about each of the component processes is more important than any of the processes on its own.

I shall attempt to explain the purposes that can be met by each process, but I shall not try to suggest quantities in which the ingredients should be mixed. Building a curriculum just isn't that kind of operation. All that C. H. Waddington has to say about the difference between modular construction and biological growth applies to the planning of education:

> The idea of a module covers two related notions: firstly, using some standard unit of length or volume as the basis for a whole design; and secondly, adopting throughout the design a single definite series of proportional relations . . . .

... in the most profound sense, biological forms can never be modular in the sense in which an architectural or pictorial design may be. It is of the essence of biological structures that they are involved in processes of growth and development. Even when we can for some purposes identify a basic unit, fundamentally it is not constant but changes (usually increases) as time passes. Similarly ... the system of proportions usually alters as development proceeds.[3]

Autonomous Studies

While we attempt to use class teaching of subjects as the only vehicle for all kinds of instruction we are forced to compromise. In any given class, interest in the subject itself varies. Some students are strongly personally attracted to the subject matter, some to the subject manner, i.e. the kind of activity allowed in studying it, and some to both, while many others have only a mild interest, and still more have none. Many would enter the subject matter with more enthusiasm if there could be greater diversity of subject manners, but the teacher is forced both by academic tradition and by timetabling to think far more of subject matter than of subject manner, and since most teachers haven't the heart to ignore most of the class completely they settle for dealing with the subject at the level of those who are only mildly interested. They have no time to enter deeply into matters with those who really care and they are able to reject altogether only a minority.

The minority are dismissed out of hand as dim or dumb. Maybe their minority membership will cover so many subjects that they will be regarded as needing remedial treatment as people, not specific coaching in the subject. In coaching we set up a tutorial situation and try on a variety of subject manners until something seems to work. This is the kind of remedial study I shall describe later on.

I described autonomous studies earlier as those directed by

teachers to a pattern determined by teachers, to meet predicted needs, to implement decisions based on other considerations than the observed needs of the students, or to meet widely observed common needs. The pattern that the teachers determine, I suggested, need not be limited by weekly timetabling of the kind now used.

I have also suggested that we could exclude from our thinking on autonomous studies the children who hate or fear the subject (coping with their needs in remedial studies) and those who have a devoted interest (coping for them with personal interest studies) so that there need be none of the time wasting that now goes on in class teaching, and autonomous studies can be conducted more efficiently and take up less time.

I now want to suggest additionally that we shift our interest from subject matter to subject manner, and use our time in autonomous studies overtly going for basic principles and not recapitulating the history of the development of the subject as a separate branch of learning. Autonomous studies in fact should be thought of as basic courses, beginning with a clearly prescribed introductory course, followed by clearly prescribed follow up courses to the level where the young are genuinely beginning to specialize and opt for personal interest studies which are designed separately from the basic courses. We can in this way eliminate the age barrier to specialization which the present system enforces and more safely use objective measurement both of the basic courses themselves and of students' success in them. Interests activated in interdisciplinary enquiry will accelerate progress through some basic courses for all youngsters, enabling some specialization for everybody carried on in mixed age groups, so that the population of specialist groups is not determined by the size of the schools' uppermost age groups. Where a youngster is held back in a basic course he has set his heart on, the remedial system comes into play to help him forward, just as it does if he has very weak command of media and needs help with seeing or hearing or walking or reading.

This approach to autonomous studies not only frees us from the five-year syllabus, which is utter nonsense as predictive planning, but it also allows us to incorporate more readily and rapidly into the planning of basic courses all the work on instruction which is already going on in schools linked to research institutes. It also allows us to catch up more nearly with the frontiers of research in the various disciplines themselves. We should not after all be teaching such antiquated oddities as "The Five Senses of Man" or be recharting phlogistian theories as science rather than as history. Only by reducing the scale of our planning can we both teach what's best of what's new and increase our instructional efficiency.

The speed at which a school can move away from class teaching as a medium for subjects towards age-free basic courses as a medium for disciplines depends of course on the speed at which it can provide a better system of remedial and personal interest specialist studies. The three are closely related by the fact that they can only emerge from a redistribution of functions at present poorly performed. But there cannot be a time when any of these functions is dropped altogether and basic courses will not work well so long as the functions are confused.

Finally I have raised one very knotty problem in talking of courses designed by teachers to implement decisions based on considerations other than the observed need of the students. On this I have very little advice to offer. All I mean to do by raising it is to acknowledge that there is a problem of conflict within schools between specialists who want to build empires because they really believe their subject is more basic than any other, and of conflict between the school and pressure groups in the community, from Black Papers to psychedelicists, from employers who want cheap exploitable young labor to the advocates of an affluent leisurely society. There will always be tension in making decisions of this kind. It is a problem which has no final solution.

However there are many components at present buried in the pudding of conventional subject disciplines which could without difficulty be brought out into the less cluttered pattern of shorter autonomous courses. Subject syllabuses are not a final solution either to the problem of understanding systems of human knowledge, problems such as the teaching of literature (submerged in English) or of economics (submerged either in history or in geography) or of cycles of transformation of energy (so deeply submerged in sciences it remains almost mythical in its cloudiness to most of us) or the ways in which energy is dispersed as matter.

If we decide that any of these is worth teaching autonomously, courses should be mounted. They will not be courses all of the same kind. The study of literature remains a matter of learning how to grasp what we need to illumine our lives by reading novels, poems, plays or other newer literary forms written by others who wrote to grasp their own lives better. It is a matter of reading at the depth indicated when we talk analogously of "reading the weather," which involves bringing all our experience to bear on our immediate experience—a way of reading which doesn't work if we are overly analytical. In this situation loss of immediacy is loss of meaning. It is a matter not of measurement, of acquaintance, not even perhaps of touch, but of *grasp*. To know how well your teaching of literature works you must see what is being seized or better still see the seizing. I have never found a better method of testing comprehension than to invite a student, who is of course known to me, simply to read aloud a poem or story he likes. The quality of the grasp is then obvious and if I want to have some dialogue on the poem I know where to begin. Just in the same way I am convinced that whenever I have been forced to lecture on poetry, my own reading of the poems has been the most effective part of what I had to say about them.

Loss of immediacy is loss of meaning. If it is not immediacy we seek in teaching literature, if we submerge it in a general process of teaching English, making it the subject matter of a notoriously matterless subject, or call it teaching language, or teaching culture or some other apology for history, we are tempted to abuse the poetry or drama by asking improper questions of it, asking it to become an illustration of something other than itself. Just in the same way we abuse museums by ignoring the things in them, treating them as if they were mere pictures of themselves put in a book to help explain a text.

There is something very "thing"-like about a good poem—less obviously so about a novel or a play but nonetheless so equally true. Each is an event, not the plan of an event.

Now it is likely that the English specialists in a school will be the best equipped to teach literature. This is *not* an argument for continuing to relate such teaching to more commonplace kinds of reading or to the analysis of advertisements (why bother anyway to insult our students by laboring the obvious?) or to teaching writing—not even to writing poetry, which ought to be a commonplace anyway, except for the few who write so well that others need what they have written, and such poetry is probably best housed in music rooms and art workshops.

An autonomous course in literature would then aim simply to create circumstances for the best possible experience of some poems, some novels, some plays and for good dialogue about our experience of them. Novels, poems, plays, happenings, dadaism, concrete verse and so on could indeed well be separated into different short courses. What in all cases must be avoided is asking stupid questions about the experience and erecting unnecessary academic superstructures.

A world of dew
Is a world of dew . . .
And yet . . . and yet.

This *haiku* is deeply Buddhist and deeply Japanese. And yet . . . is it not everybody's experience of repudiating the world as reality—a necessary defense against the inevitability of our eventually losing it? I don't think any commentary on the origins of that *haiku* is capable of adding anything to it.

A basic course in economics would have of course to be quite differently structured. In teaching literature the teacher is finding what he can in common with his students and an author. The investigation is itself immediate experience. The text is present not as a representative of something somewhere else but as the very thing being explored. Economics calls for the study of more distant events which have to be grasped through representation. The first problem, determined by and determining the conceptualization of that set of human relationships we call economic, is one of selection of data to be presented by the teacher.

The fault of most teaching of economics at a rudimentary level (not escaped much higher up alas) is that it fails to challenge the conventions of data collection which have arisen in the evolution of economics as a utilitarian social science. Since it is by no means certain what data are economically relevant, and this is the major problem of economics as a discipline, I would be tempted, and certainly succumb, to tackle the problem of improving economic understanding in a way which could lead to a more disciplined study of economics by adopting a thematic approach and set up a course on poverty. In this I would compare poverty in our own industrial society (enforcing wherever possible some fieldwork which involves meeting poor people and getting to know how they see their own plight) with poverties in the exploited "Third World," also looking at what is happening to peoples now being turned into poor natives by the intrusion of petrol and mining interests into cultures which had managed until now to be isolated, as in New Guinea.

In such a course some questions would have to be raised about the nature of functionary divisions of labor and its effect on people's perception of each other; about the acceleration of men's use of resources; the effect on our reservoirs of energy of the strange phenomenon that not only does world population increase, but as it increases each human being demands, in order to avoid poverty, to use much more energy in his lifetime than individuals did a generation ago. I am told that Indian villagers watched "lazily" while a young, fresh, strong American volunteer worker dug a well for them. They watched not with admiration but with apprehension. What alarmed them was the question "How much will he have to eat to be able to work like that?" They knew the answer would be "More than any dozen of us." This is economic data of the kind that has to be brought in if the phenomenon of poverty is to be understood. The question of aid to underdeveloped countries would have to be raised too, and would have to be handled in such ways as to allow exploration of such assertions as I heard Mr. Neville

Kanakaratne, Economic Minister for Ceylon in London, make at a public meeting, that if Ceylon could get one new penny a pound more for her tea (out of the wide margin of market profit, not from the consumer) she would need no economic aid from anybody.

Data for such a study could be collected readily from the representatives in Britain of poor countries and from the press, supplemented by pamphlets from the agencies involved in aid programs especially, in Britain, from the Child Poverty Action Group for poverty on our doorsteps and from Christian Aid and Oxfam for poverties abroad. Both agencies continually collect and publish up-to-date information, some freely and all cheaply.

I would argue that an autonomous course of study of poverty is essential for our adolescents anyway. There is no making sense of the international affairs of the world they live in without an explanation of poverty and the economic systems which are failing to cope with it. But there must be no preaching or whitewashing the failure.

The same could be said of the basic scientific riddle of energy/matter—what kind of energy system is our universe? where are we *as energy* within it?—and of basic knowledge of human biology.

It is of little use for any school to wait for textbooks to arrive on the scene to solve this problem of designing well pro-grammed short autonomous courses externally. The work going on in programming courses by subsidized agencies (especially the Schools Council and Nuffield projects in Britain, EDC in the United States) is providing some useful, and rather more dubious, structured programs. The best of such projects are those designed for the shortest term use, and are useful as models. But quite the most rapid way to get a collection of data to use in structured courses is to set up your own scanning and press-cutting service in the school. Give each student a highly specific topic to collect and have all students from time to time pass round and cut out newspapers, magazines and journals collected at regular intervals from any neighbors who will keep back issues. Subscribe to any useful journals which can't be had free. Stick the cuttings on card and keep them in stout transparent plastic envelopes so that they will last. In this way data accumulates very quickly. The useful areas of dead textbooks can also be cut out and kept in the same way, as can pictures and work cards or cards or provocative questions.

Such scanning can be used with all levels where the students can read or even with pictures where the children cannot. To be involved in scanning is to be preparing for a vital rapidly growing modern trade as well as finding a good use for the skill of reading.

Remedial Studies

It is quite widely acknowledged that the commonest cause of backwardness is the label itself. However disadvantaged anybody may be by being born into a cultural minority, it is not the accident of birth nor the membership of the minority that closes the door to personal development. It is the act performed by people who tell you the door is closed which bars your way. Even to be told that you ought to try the back door or the tradesman's entrance is to be told quite clearly that there is something wrong with you. Neil Warren, making a very wide and thorough survey of the population of a Los Angeles suburb, concluded that:

> ... most of those who are labelled retarded could be classified as moderately or mildly handicapped ... These are the "educable" retarded who are expected to profit from special classes or programs. It is this group for which the label is most critical. There is evidence that if someone in this range for some reason is not labelled before he becomes an adult, he may never acquire the label at all. He may blend into the community without too great difficulty and perform a role that is reasonably useful to society and satisfying to himself.[4]

I have already indicated my belief that the gap between performances in school and real life performance is so great that no relationship can be held to exist between them, except insofar as a youngster may be so discouraged by the way he is put down in school that all normal social ambition is sapped in him, so that he doesn't attempt work he could easily master, nor of course aim to exercise the social influence which is his right. Convenient as all this may be to an autocratic society, it is highly dangerous to democracy. It becomes especially important therefore to rid our schools of any traces of such blanket labelling. In any case to use it is to defeat what we take to be our aims with any remedial system which is to help development. Special remedial classes for a minority are no help.

> Does the majority affix the label of mental retardation merely to those who fail to conform to its standards? The humanitarian desire to help the less capable members of our society may actually lead us to attach a stigma that does more harm than good.[5]

I take this matter to be an acutely urgent one. As the size of population increases so the size of every minority increases and confrontations of minorities on the frontiers of justice, of fair and equable distribution of human rights becomes rapidly more sensitive a political issue. Any society that means to be whole must act to ensure its wholeness. Emergent racialism in Britain, breeding still more stereotypes of "backwardness" along with the proliferation of typecasting systems invented by mechanistic psychologists, splits us further and further from each other. The practice of setting up long-term remedial classes or even remedial streams in schools enforces divisions, enforces stereotypes and enforces failure on the stereotyped young. And the job said to be done by this kindly separation is never in fact done. A large secondary school is likely to have a head of remedial department and he is likely to be a good, devoted and highly professional teacher. But he is most unlikely to have an equally highly professional staff. The position is the one we find at every leaking joint of the Welfare State. Even if the job could be done in that way by very special treatment for the disadvantaged or inadequate, there are never enough people around to do such a job and there never will be. The realities are those Gordon Bowker points to:

It is worth noting too that because many multiracial schools are to be found in downtown areas, and suffer from a high staff turnover, there is also likely to be a higher than usual number of what might be called "marginal" teachers, those engaged in supply teaching, relieving a temporary staff shortage. These teachers may well be quite uninvolved in what they are doing in the school and the role which they prefer to define for themselves may be quite other than that of teacher, either academic or child centred.[6]

Yet there are cultural disadvantages and there are personal disabilities from other sources. Everybody has some disabilities and we do need a system for helping people to overcome them.

But to talk of disabilities at all is to admit that we have a picture of the nature of abilities. All attempts so far this century to locate this picture in theories of intelligence having failed and with new abilities being called for anyway by rapid changes of the human condition, we are left no guidelines for prediction in this matter. We are back to the problem I left unresolved at the end of the last chapter. In matters of remedial education I think it boils down to accepting that all our measurements must be relative to the individual and not to any absolute standards. If a man loses a leg or suffers a stroke, we concern ourselves from day to day with how much improvement there is in his mobility. It isn't just a question of can he walk or not walk, but a matter of how much improvement can slowly be made. The same I think applies to all remedial measures.

Since any apparent overall backwardness is most likely to turn out to be the result of a kind of social poverty, an inability to offer to be involved, we must use interdisciplinary enquiry groupings to help the youngster find gifts that will be received by his fellows and let him spend a lot of time in this process, giving perhaps less time to basic courses of autonomous studies and more time to specifically remedial help with baffling elements of the basic courses so that they can be planned and so that the collaborative process can be used. The "bright" child trying maths and floundering can work with the "dim" child floundering at more than maths. Much of the remedial work can be programmed to be used by clusters with tutorial advice from teachers, and the process can be controlled by skilled remedial teachers acting as first stop consultants and diagnosticians, but also acting as the channel towards more expert advice from outside the school. The remedial teachers are needed also of course to play a peripatetic part in focus group work, helping in decisions about how any cluster's enquiry should go forward, and acting as consultants to every child's personal tutor about balancing the total work schedule which becomes the basis of all timetabling.

Special Interest Studies

It is into this process that most of what academic teachers would call "real teaching" is displaced. If a specialist is of any value to the young at all, it is because he is expert and is committed to the learning his discipline represents. In most of our teaching in secondary schools as we find them, few of us are able to allow ourselves that commitment and so much of our time is spent in avoiding the glazed eyes of bored children, or hopelessly putting up a defense against the open challenge "What *use* is all this?"

Special interest studies gives equal importance to what the youngsters themselves nominate as worth studying and what the teachers find most worthwhile. As the purpose is to arrange a meeting of like interests, the conditions for collaborative learning can be met without conflict, so long as the youngsters feel the process exists for their sake and is not a Trojan Horse sneaked in to give more territory to the basic courses of autonomous studies. It includes all sorts of sports and games which can be raised to the power of specialist studies, as well as the old academic and artistic pursuits. It may very well be that the pressure to succeed in public examinations may influence both the nomination of choices and the energy put into study but that, I take it, is no bad thing.

Since it is intended that groups shall be composed with as little forcing of choice as possible and with no lower age limit to entry, it is within the teacher's right to accept or refuse entry to a group depending on his assessment of personal ability to cope with the studies. This suggests a need to provide a considerable variety of kinds of special interest studies. Many adolescent interests turn out to be ephemeral, even faddish, so this has to be allowed for and the right to drop out has to be extended. At the same time teachers will not set up an elaborate course for students who are unlikely to apply themselves, so both serious continuing courses and sampling courses are needed in disciplines that genuinely demand structured sequential planning. It could well be that for such disciplines, success in a basic course of autonomous study should be made the entry condition. In others of course there is no need for such structuring. One provides the opportunity to play football, and one offers a criticism of the game. Those who just want to play without thinking seriously of improving can go on playing that kind of game. Those who want to master the art can play more rigorously and study the art of football. Some who can't play well may still have a keen technical interest in the game and they should be treated as serious students too. In fact some could attend the theoretical sessions without ever practising the game and others of course need have nothing to do with football at all.

The range of skills available amongst the staff and other members of the school should not determine the range of choices. What the school cannot provide should be sought elsewhere. It may indeed be necessary to systematize this across all the schools in an area. A youngster would retain membership of his school and go elsewhere only for specialist studies. This would certainly be preferable to yet another stage of education in the form of sixth form colleges or any other precollegiate institution.

Nor should we aim to load the brightest youngsters with more work than the others. It is still not unheard of for a headmaster to *boast* that a pupil has been induced to get thirteen O levels. The school I suppose gets some kudos from a raw score of exam successes but it has no educational meaning and the effort involved for the youngster is a waste of life. Scores of this kind should be kept to the wonder world of pinball machines. To demand that a youngster follows up everything he shows any sign of being good at rather than allowing him to express this competence in the depth and scope of his interdisciplinary enquiries inevitably overloads and confuses him. The genuinely fascinating personal specialist study suffers too; the potentially inventive student becomes instead a drudge in his best field.

And anyway schooling isn't everything is it? A world in which only the dim or the sixteen-year-old dropouts have time to go courting is very dull and nasty.

Assessments and Organization

One thing I do not need to be told at this stage is that I have not been describing a school that anyone can recognize. To many teachers such a curriculum as I have outlined will seem simply incomprehensible. The reader is being forced to play detective. What's happened to registration? What's happened to the mark book? Where's algebra gone? Whatever happened to Babylon?

Fair enough. My description has been predictive, built by projection from my knowledge of the problems of organization now being met by teachers who, having changed *some* elements of the structure of schooling, find that other elements have to be changed too. Most of all they find that any change which demands a change of attitude demands also the rejection of commonly current procedures, some of which can simply be dropped but others of which have to be replaced by something new. What is certain is that we cannot simply go on adding new demands to the old ones. Teachers are already terribly overburdened beasts, spending far too much of their time buried under paperwork. So what stays, what changes and what disappears from the school's administrative procedures? Again I rely for my answers on my predictions. Obviously not all the changes I am going to suggest can happen at the same time, so I will outline a strategy for bringing all the necessary changes about at the end of the chapter.

What stays? First, subject specialist teachers, because they are the best means at present of making varied expertise available to the youngsters. Of course this means retaining some structure in subject departments although that will no longer dominate the structure of the curriculum. Second, year grouping as the basic division of the school's student population, although age barriers may be dissolved more or less in all the four processes of the curriculum. Third, each teacher will have a special responsibility for particular children, though he may now fulfil this responsibility as a personal tutor to a mixed age group rather than as a form master. He will be administratively responsible to the head for keeping such records about each child as may be deemed necessary and for advising each student about the composition of work schedules. He is also responsible for all that has been meant by pastoral care.

What changes? First, observation replaces assessment except in matters of success in clearly designed basic courses of autonomous studies. We stop pretending to measure success with inadequate instruments and record our observations of what happened instead, as far as we feel a need to, so the system of records changes and face to face discussion of students' performance replaces paper work. Second, publication of all reports on students changes to narrative statement of major improvements and the amount of reporting done is cut back to the level actually needed. Reports are composed if demanded by parents or others who have a right to ask instead of as a matter of course at regular intervals. The mode of publication chosen should be as authentic as possible, discussion always being preferable to a questionnaire or form. Third, changes should be brought about in the system of public examinations to conform with this policy of observation rather than assessment. Fourth, the role of the head or principal changes from that of a centralizing director to that of a decentralizing facilitator who occupies himself helping his staff to fulfil their new roles.

What disappears altogether? First, all regular internal school examinations. Some testing may be appropriate in measuring success in phases of autonomous study and some diagnostic tests may be helpful in making decisions about remedial studies, but these should be objective tests, not tests devised to enable the publishing of rank orders. All mark lists disappear into the personal tutor's files. Second, the class as a basic group must go and with it all streaming. If streaming is retained to any extent it should only be in the initial stage of changeover from long-term syllabus subject teaching to short-term autonomous study courses. Third, the centralized control of timetable disappears. Timing instead becomes a matter of negotiation and the head of course retains responsibility for resolving disputes, but he no longer governs the distribution of teachers to classes at preordained times. He can of course give this responsibility to somebody else but a central clearing house is needed. Fourth, bells, Tannoy systems, prefects and all the other clutter of media for centralized control, all of which exist only to serve the timetable, will no longer be needed. Fifth, the perpetual supervision of youngsters by teachers is eliminated. Much of the work in all four processes will be done in clusters and all pupils will be more often working with their fellows than with a teacher.

The administration is thus decentralized. The centre is the collective role of all members of the staff as personal tutors and there is no reason why the head should not share in this. Every teacher has the same variety of responsibilities as member of a focus group, as organizer of some autonomous, some remedial and some special interest courses and as a personal tutor. The load at present carried by some two-thirds of the staff who as form teachers register groups of thirty or forty youngsters is redistributed evenly. Some teachers have the heavier load of leading their subject departments or of leading the reform of remedial methods. Some may lead groups of personal tutors in a house system, but these are burdens that already exist so nothing is being added. The new system, being debureaucratized, should in fact be easier to administer. Significant decisions have to be made more frequently it is true, but then far more people share the making of them.

More people should also be involved in keeping records. The best authentic system will be one based on each pupil's own record and assessment of his own achievement, supplemented by teachers' comments and records of results of objective tests where they are relevant. This system, which evolves in inter-disciplinary enquiry as a way of sorting out who does what in the work of each cluster, can be elaborated and extended to cover all work and activities.

Phasing the Changeover to a Fourfold Curriculum

Given that the starting point is a conventional secondary school organization of streamed classes following a subject teaching timetable, with two administrative channels—registration of attendance and so on by a form teacher and pastoral care by tutors in a house system—there should be both a preparatory phase to establish more *common* experience for all members of the school and a simplification of the administration.

Preparatory Phase

Centre all administration on tutors handling mixed age groups. All pupils report to their tutor at beginning of school day, discuss common school business and any personal private business, or make appointments for later discussion. Once this system is established, have the tutors draw up lists of personal interest studies their charges wish to undertake, and give up some school time to such projects. The groupings should be determined solely by interest so that groups mixed in age and ability may develop and extend beyond the school boundaries. Involve parents and neighbors. Let all parties get used to personal responsibility for work undertaken. All follow-up is through the tutor, not whoever is running a personal interest studies group.

The tutor keeps copies of work schedules and discusses strategic problems. This process is meant to assist in a shift towards more authentic relationships throughout the school as well as strengthening pastoral care and beginning to break down age and streaming barriers. The extra time which will be needed will mean that something will have to be reduced in the subject timetabling but perhaps fewer school assemblies need be held. The shift of all administration to a tutorial organization enables a later shift to be made to setting groups rather than streaming classes for subject teaching, without committing the school to a hasty abandonment of class teaching as its chief medium of instruction. It opens the way to a change of attitudes towards the role of autonomous studies rather than trying to enforce change. Without these preparations (which in any case are improvements in basic organization and pastoral care) which gradually introduce the personal interest studies process for the whole school before introducing interdisciplinary enquiry for some of it, there is much more likelihood of genuine conflicts of interest arising in the following phases.

First Phase

Set up focus groups for interdisciplinary enquiry to handle incoming first year pupils and possibly nonacademic older pupils too. Distribute the children to personal tutors and let these do any initial interviewing, and receive groups of children from primary schools at intervals throughout the term before they join the school. Let the children also meet their focus groups so that they will understand how they will be working.

If it is possible to offer these first year pupils a system of autonomous studies in the form of basic courses rather than subject teaching, do so. Since this shift is the most difficult of all the transitions to make, it should not be hurried. At this stage all the staff are involved in learning the new role of personal tutor and some direction of special interest studies. A few are additionally learning to act as a focus group and some of their colleagues are acting occasionally as consultants. To try to add in an extra demand for decisions which call for careful thinking by the whole of each subject department could very well overload the whole staff.

Nevertheless preparations should begin for building up a new system of records and an index of resources. The new system of records has to be agreed by the staff as a whole or it will not work. Only through lengthy, informal and leisurely discussion will a new common view of purposes be discovered and our view of our purposes decides what we will bother to record, as indeed it decides what we notice about the students.

Building an index of resources is the quickest way to see what is available in the school and what will be needed initially to provide for interdisciplinary enquiry, but in the long run for autonomous studies too. The time to move over to autonomous studies is whenever the teachers are familiar with the full range of resources which could be used in structuring courses.

Second Phase

Extend interdisciplinary enquiry by composing new focus groups to take on the second year pupils who will themselves be used to the process, having used it in their first year, and to cover general studies at sixth form level. Perhaps institute one of the more structured modes of enquiry for fourth and fifth year pupils, planning it to result in Mode 3 CSE courses.

Give the pupils responsibility for keeping work schedules in consultation with their personal tutors and set up a remedial studies service for first and second year pupils but not necessarily limited to them.

This phase may take at least two years. It is ended when the whole school is using to some extent three processes—interdisciplinary enquiry, remedial and special interest studies—but the final shift from subject teaching to structured courses of autonomous studies has not been accomplished. This is the only process which is really affected by external demands—the policy of examining bodies, the entry requirements of industries and further education—so it may have to wait on shifts in other areas or be achieved by compromise.

Final Phase

Set up autonomous studies as clearly demarcated and structured courses, breaking away altogether from long-term syllabus planning.

Summary

1. Interdisciplinary enquiry does not replace anything in the present curriculum. Its purpose is not instructional and it is not alternative to integrated studies or projects. Its claim to exist in schools is that it is the way of learning most appropriate to adolescents.
2. Instructional class teaching as a medium is inevitably inefficient because it confuses a number of functions which would best be redistributed into other processes. It also causes streaming, which is a damaging way of trying to make class instruction efficient.
3. Autonomous studies can take over the central function of class teaching (instruction) but only if it is restructured as a series of clear-cut courses with short-term objectives. Current subject boundaries may turn out to be too widely drawn to be appropriate to autonomous studies.
4. Remedial studies should be systematically provided for all students as needed and the remedies should be specific, not general. There should be no composition of permanent remedial groups separated from other students.
5. Special interest studies should be set up to cover both ephemeral and lasting interests of the students and cater for mixed age groups. The range should include academic and artistic specialization as well as all manner of games, hobbies and other pursuits.
6. Administration should be decentralized and the whole staff should be involved as personal tutors in bearing the load of administration and pastoral care which is normally borne only by form masters. The personal tutor should carry responsibility for his students' work schedules, records, and

care, in collaboration with his students. Tutors and students could be grouped in houses in large schools.

7. At present schools are structures needing modification. The aim is to convert them to systems of an organic kind which cope readily with change as a matter of course. Any moves towards a fourfold curriculum must therefore be seen as moves which will cause more changes later on and some initial strategy should be worked out to enable change to go on smoothly over a period of years.

References

1. John Cage, "Rhythm etc," in *Module, Symmetry, Proportion,* Gyorgy Kepes, ed. (Studio Vista, 1966).
2. See note 1 above.
3. C. H. Waddington, "The Modular Principle and Biological Form," in *Module, Symmetry, Proportion*, Gyorgy Kepes, ed. (Studio Vista, 1966).
4. Neil D. Warren, "Who are the Backward?" in *New Society* (August 28, 1969).
5. See note 4 above.
6. Gordon Bowker, *Education of Coloured Immigrants* (Longmans Green, 1968; Humanities Press, 1969).

CHAPTER 7

Changing Our Teaching

Redesigning an educational system is a relatively easy exercise.
Changing one's own teaching, especially when it has been
acclaimed as successful by all the old standards, is very much
harder. To the outsider it may be obvious that most of what
goes on in schools is relevant only to schools, that the system
itself is composed of routines which guarantee the success of
self-fulfilling prophecies and that trivia has been elevated to fill
the place left empty in modern life by really meaningful rituals.
But for the teacher these rituals and routines are defenses of a
most important kind. We cling to them because we need them.
They enable us to work numbly, without feeling, and without
having to reveal to ourselves the sense of panic which drives us
through much of our most tedious work.

Nostalgia, as some anonymous graffittist wrote, ain't what it
used to be. But when I look back, trying to discover what it was
that brought me into teaching rather than into some other
trade, I must confess a lot of nostalgia got into the decision,
along with a lot of honest emotional commitment. To a large
extent I was looking to perpetuate the only successes I had in
adolescence which were of an academic and aesthetic kind.
Outside school life was too dangerous for me. I didn't cope any

too well with my peer group anyway except in fairly formal circumstances. Out of school I spent a lot of my time in a youth club, and a little later in political committees.

The only thing I was fortunate in was the ease with which adults accepted me and enjoyed what seemed to be my nonconformity (which now as I look back seems to have been a very conventional piece of role playing of rebellious youth, tight rope walking in search of a self). I didn't find myself but I did learn how to manipulate people. My peers found me too bossy and they were right. It has taken years to diminish that bossiness, and it certainly took years of teaching before I began to recognize that I was spending my life dominating others by manipulating them, usually with the charm I had acquired in adolescence but I had a Machiavellian shrewdness in reserve which could be used if need be. I was promoted much too rapidly, not only because I was thought to be a good teacher but also because I was a good controller of people. This, I came to recognize, was what I was being paid for—and quite well paid too.

When you get to the top and spend much of your time manipulating governors and education officers of the bureaucratic kind (there are some others—a few honorable exceptions) you are left in little doubt that your first job is to keep things quiet, keep things running smoothly and that you will have official support for fairly violent shows of brute strength if you think they are needed to keep the young in line. Magistrates aren't allowed to order the flogging of a youngster; but they will very rarely fail to exonerate the teacher who flogs a youngster if the latter's parents sue him for assault. Power always depends in the long run on physical force but of course it has to be avoided if possible. We control by manipulation if we can and a sound routine controls both our clients and ourselves.

Yet teachers do have feelings and their fundamental feelings are as hostile to the routine of our secondary schools as the youngsters' feelings are. The most tragic aspect of the whole business is that most teachers are genuinely idealistic and put up with poor pay and quite scandalous conditions of work because they really want to help the young forward. Even those (and they are many) who come into teaching because they have been forced to study in a college of education by a shortage of university places, at some point decide the job is worth doing and stick at it only for that reason. As students, would-be teachers are the most restricted and the least rebellious. They are worked incredibly hard, expected to cope with studying psychology of and philosophy of and sociology of education (the greatest nondiscipline of all as it is taught) as well as becoming proficient specialists in some subject. Their study is interrupted rather than supported by traumatic experiences of class teaching practice in which the thing that worries them most is not whether they are actually teaching anything, but whether they are getting by from day to day without losing control. They are expected to be able to explain the educational purpose of every move they make and justify it (no wonder the objectives nonsense has become a major industry) and they are clearly marked as second rate students not only by being asked to carry double the work load of other students, but by getting inferior grants to support them.

All this the student has to cope with without the massive supports I had from growing up in wartime when the nation shared a sense of purpose which was convincing; when the imminence of death broke through the taboos on unpleasant reality which operate in peace time, so that our value system was more fully human; when nobody could make pretenses that man's inhumanity to man is an occasional freak behavior rather than a standing danger. It was easier for me to build the values that have eventually enabled me to quarrel with the system, growing up among people who had genuine commitment and a sense of community that transcended subcultures and included anyone who wanted to join the struggle. I was even able to begin my teaching by taking a part time job in a progressive boarding school which had among its pupils many who had been rescued from Nazi concentration camps. Many of my teachers were my friends, without barriers. My schooling was frequently interrupted as the school had to cope with evacuees from Birmingham and routine was very light anyway. The sixth form was small and all teaching was intimate and tutorial.

As long as we recruit most of our teachers from people who have been forced to make their choice in late adolescence, we shall go on having a severe problem of changing our teaching. The impersonality of university and college of education teaching is even more damaging that the impersonality of our schools which is already much worse than it was only one generation ago.

It takes personal courage to resist and fight and change a system which has general social support as our secondary schooling system has. Most of the demands for change which are being made and the most popular reasons given are all expedient, matters of economics. These are not good enough reasons to motivate change. The energy will only come from those who want to change our schools because they recognize their systematic inhumanity and see *that* (as well as all its other manifestations in society, including the destruction of the environment) as a crisis demanding as much mobilization of commitment as did the war in which I grew up.

I am not merely declaiming as our pupils do against a simple lack of enthusiasm in most teaching. I think that most teachers are idealistic and are in the profession because they are capable of commitment; that they are even seeking a community, rather than cause, to commit themselves to. And the danger is not that men are born enthusiasts, however restrained, but that if we do not become enthusiasts for life, we become enthusiasts for death or enthusiasts for order. The aggressive instinct can manifest itself either in genuine community building or in destruction or in building phoney communities where violation of life is used as the weapon instead of overt violence. Where we find, as I am sure we do in teaching, that we allow ourselves to violate ourselves and spend our days in excusing or justifying our conduct rather than in simply, enthusiastically enjoying our work, we are destroying more than we build.

I may be oversensitive on this issue, confessing a personal sense of guilt at much of what I did as a secondary school teacher. But I think my account of things is accurate from what I have learned from the teachers I have worked most closely with and from the amounts of time I have seen others devote to making excuses, and to engineering battles among themselves in the staff room and with pupils in the classroom.

I know of only one way through this problem—and it has to be a way through, not a way round. We have to be freed to teach enthusiastically without making excuses. The school has to become a place where authentic community can be enjoyed. I don't think it matters that teachers work in schools because they are seeking a community they cannot find elsewhere in our society. After all it doesn't exist elsewhere in society, so I can't see what harm would be done by making a better community in school than we now have. The sense of community is something the young need too, community with adults. To be left with concepts of society and no sense of community is to suffer the final violation.

Lorenz puts all this more powerfully:

It would seem that once the sensitive period has elapsed, a man's ability to embrace ideals at all is considerably reduced .... It determines neither more nor less than that which a man will live for .... Without the concentrated dedication of militant enthusiasm neither art nor science, nor indeed any of the great endeavours of humanity would ever have come into being. Whether enthusiasm is made to serve these endeavours, or whether man's most powerfully motivating instinct makes him go to war in some abjectly silly cause, depends almost entirely on the conditioning and/or imprinting he has undergone during certain susceptible periods of his life. There is reasonable hope that our moral responsibility may gain control over the primeval drive, but our only hope of it ever doing so rests on the humble recognition of the fact that militant enthusiasm is an instinctive response with a phylogenetically determined releasing mechanism and the only point at which intelligent and responsible supervision can get control is in the

175

conditioning of the response to an object which has proved
to be a genuine value.[1]

Of course one can't discuss the genuineness of values with
people who don't share them. This is what makes all the
difficulties in the education of teachers as teachers and what
makes it almost impossible for me to *write* about all this. My
way of working is the result of months of talking and sharing
experience, the result of a patient process of coming to know
other people slowly and working with them in a designedly
debureaucratized set up.

But then the whole purpose of this book has been to explore
ways of debureaucratizing schools, of moving again towards
authenticity of relationship, so that the young and the teachers
can come patiently to know each other and work together. I
have said enough about the kind of relationship the young need
with us and the importance of clustering rather than massing.
What matters now is to picture the relationships teachers could
have with each other and with other adults.

Sociological study of schools as social systems is fairly new
trade but it is already becoming a truism that conflicts between
teachers mostly arise from a clash of two kinds of teacher
personality, the authoritarian and the child centred. Having
observed that very often the teachers who talk authoritarian
establish more authentic relationships than many who talk child
centred, I would rather look elsewhere into the anticollabora-
tive structure of the system and into the anomalous demand
that teachers should have such a thing as a teacher personality
anyway rather than just a person personality. Such a demand
obviously is made but who or what makes it?

Certainly part of the demand comes from within, from the
nostalgia I have already referred to, the great likelihood that we
model ourselves on what we took to be the personality of some
of our own teachers whom we admired or feared and that this
modelling has not been modified in the interval between being a
pupil and being a teacher. I can't see any other possible
explanation for the fact that all the teaching that goes on in

teacher training colleges has absolutely no effect at all on what young teachers do in school. A very small minority actually perceive the role of a teacher differently as a result of studying education.

But more important still, and more influential, is the notion that there is such a thing as "the teacher's role" which can be discerned and described and played. I would hesitate, to say the least, to go on stage to play Lear with my adolescent essays on the role in my hand. We don't hesitate to ask young teachers to see what they are doing in school as a kind of play acting. Of course, that isn't what the sociologist means by role but most people survive "Soc. of Ed." courses with the play-acting connotations of the term undisturbed.

Worse yet, the sociological use of the term "role" does refer to a kind of play acting even where sociologists say it doesn't. It is wishful thinking when they imagine they can give the word a definition which excludes its earliest meaning. Wherever we talk of people filling a role we are talking of a way of playing a part and where we extend the term to nonpeople and talk of the role of law in society and so on we are reverting to allegory, the personification of mystery plays and the pageantry of primeval drama.

This would be of little importance in a trade geared to the production of consumer goods because however bad the effects on the worker and on his productivity, the product itself is not affected by his view of himself as playing a role. But it plays havoc with all professions where authenticity of relationship affects what decisions are made, what gets done and how. The best times of life—the times that feel most authentic—are the times when we get *out* of role, lose any sensation of play acting and act as selves. The breakdown of community into society passes the danger mark when the division of labor into specialist productive functions, which may be held to make sense economically, is extended into a community's central collaborative work of maintaining itself as a community. To replace conscience and custom by law and policemen, to replace normal human care and concern by welfare officers, to replace knowing how society works by professional sociologists, knowing about

177

people and their human feelings by professional psychologists, and to replace the experience of growing up, seeing what people must do to survive and enjoy life, by professional teachers actively destroys society. What should be the social basis—interactions of people all doing the same living and helping each other understand it—becomes a difficult matter of communication between specialists who protect their possession of some fragmented part of life by special language and special procedures.

Adolescents in the world as it is *must* use their teachers somehow to achieve their own identity. Role is not identity. If teachers of adolescents particularly cannot escape from play acting and be real in their everyday work, the most important part of their job cannot be done. If the young cannot learn with us they certainly cannot learn from us.

Yet the secondary school is the most highly bureaucratized of all our institutions. What the teacher does is governed by competition with his fellows, separation of functions and a series of grids—the class register, the timetable, the mark book, the syllabus, and report forms of various kinds. His output is measured in paper returns and his financial value measured in rank order in a subject teaching hierarchy. How can we pretend to relate authenticity to people, young or old, in such a system?

Without recounting any of the many horror stories of cases of simple mistaken identity which we all know happen even in small schools, I would suggest that any teacher who thinks my account of the falseness of relationship accepted as authentic knowledge in schools is exaggerated try a couple of experiments, recommended to me by Philip Jackson.

Make up a pack of name cards for a class you teach. At the end of some day in which you have taught that class, sit down with the cards and divide them into two groups: the children who spoke to you and those who didn't. Think of other categories of behavior in the classroom and divide the cards into packs for them too. How many children do you find you can't place at all? And how many categories have you been able to think of anyway? This will begin to tell you how much you actually notice the young you are teaching.

Another more difficult version of this selftesting is to work without a list of names to prompt you. Write down all the youngsters you have taught in the last lesson, one at a time, noting briefly all you know of each one before you begin on the next. When you have finished your list, check to see how many you forgot altogether and then try to work out why the list you have made has the order it has. Then if you have the strength go further. How many of these youngsters' parents do you know to the extent of being able to put a face to the name? How many of them do you know anything about reliably? How big are the families? Where do they live? How many children do you teach in a week? What do they know about you? What have you actually told them about yourself? What do you expect them to gather? What do you know about yourself that you wish them *not* to know? Are there things you let your colleagues know that you wouldn't let the pupils know? How many of your colleagues do you hate? How many of them do you not know at all?

If you find the experience of questioning yourself in this way disturbing or humiliating, don't blame yourself. The fault is in the system, much of it even in the simple demand that we teach classes. Put any human being in front of rows of human eyes and the barriers go up. They have to. It is a dangerously exposed position to occupy. Even the smallest secondary school has too large a staff to make a good working group which can fully collaborate; one just doesn't expect to relate at all fully to more than a handful of one's colleagues.

Probably the greatest advantage of the collaborative processes built into the fourfold curriculum for teachers is that there is less demand to spend one's time isolated in control of a class and more time spent working in a small focus group opportunistically engaged in interdisciplinary enquiry, or in a tutorial relationship with the young. These are circumstances which encourage authenticity, allow a more relaxed personal style of teaching and diminish the threat which we all feel when overexposed to too many people. By relaxing the timetable and including everybody far more in making decisions, the system loosens the hierarchy of the staffroom. It can thus reduce the competitive element in relationship with colleagues to a more manageable level. Nothing I think can ever eliminate it, but competitiveness is only a danger when it vitiates any chance of effective collaborations.

The system also of course allows a different kind of specialization. In a focus group those who hate lecturing can avoid any occasion for it; those who enjoy it can still do it. Teachers who dislike contact can concentrate on producing better focussed courses of autonomous studies and act as consultants without trying to work directly in interdisciplinary enquiry as members of focus groups. Personality has more play in the possibility of choosing the social medium in which you want to teach. The business of managing a class no longer dominates teaching life.

The system also allows for much more working liaison with outsiders, including parents, and this allows teachers to meet others and come to welcome their influence in the school without the formalities of arbitrarily arranged meetings whose very formality excludes the neighboring society from schools at present. Why should parents or anybody come into our schools merely to be told what we want of them, knowing that they are not going to be allowed to participate or otherwise influence us?

I shall not pursue the implications of what I have had to say so far about teacher training. I think they are obvious. In Britain at least the business is scandalously mismanaged. The whole financing and staffing of colleges of education (remember we don't *train* teachers any more—we *educate* them now) depends on fluctuating estimates from year to year of the demand for teachers three years hence. There is no allowance for wastage. We do not select entrants on the basis of their likely happiness in teaching. We do nothing effectively to help them find themselves through the education we offer them. We talk a lot about it. We say that education does that for them anyway but it quite obviously doesn't. Again a faulty system cancels some very well meant and even passionate efforts. There are some excellent departments in every college but no college that could be said to concern itself deeply with helping the young teacher achieve authenticity.

Nor does the quality of the teaching offered make lifelong learners of the students. The experience offered of most disciplines is more off-putting than exciting. It consists mostly of gathering information and is syllabus driven. Yet what I have said earlier about the need for teachers to go on learning all their lives and the danger of losing track of new developments in their own specialties is real. Teachers who do not have a genuine skill in learning and enthusiasm for learning (not just a nervous response to a fear of suffering professionally from getting out of date) are even more useless now than they were in the past.

The answer of course is to build a collaborative system in which schools and colleges merge, share and exchange staff to help students learn their art of teaching collaboratively with teachers. But this runs counter to the hierarchic traditions of the profession and the entrenched authoritarianism of many faculties of our universities, as well as the parsimonious traditions of the Treasury and the lack of courage of governments whenever progress wants to overturn old applecarts.

Still, there are many teachers. If government is unlikely to initiate and finance new collaborations there is no need to wait. There are enough teachers to make a very large pressure group if only they will determine to discuss education as well as the problems of teachers' rewards, and the institutions already provided as teachers' meeting grounds could be taken over in the interests of education. Some teachers' centres for instance, staffed by overworked and underpaid part time organizers, are already doing very exciting work. If an authority is lagging behind in providing centres, teachers have a right to ask and a right to influence policy. Much as can be done in any school to improve schooling there, a more general improvement will come only when the selfcontainment of schools is broken down and teachers show a readiness to meet each other and learn from each other. There really are no experts in our business but ourselves.

It is when men stop looking for leaders that they begin to be competent democrats.

Summary

1. Most teachers are driven into the profession not by a desire to escape from the world outside, but by idealism, an attachment to values they first found as adolescents modelling themselves on teachers.
2. This makes it difficult for teachers objectively to criticize the system they work in. Nevertheless the system prevents them from expressing their ideals effectively.
3. Excessive attachment to rigid order can be produced by confinement in systems which prevent aggression from being properly used in building and maintaining community.
4. Secondary schools at present are systems of that kind. Timetables do a prison make, and classroom walls a cage. This increases the difficulty for most teachers in deciding to reject the system.
5. Nevertheless teachers do have a genuine high valuation of community and this would find better expression in a system founded on authenticity of relationships.
6. Preparation of students for teaching is inadequate especially because it is impersonal. It imitates the secondary school system, allowing scarcely more freedom and initiative to the student, and so reinforces the students' attachment to the system even where it preaches the urgency of change.
7. If change does not come from serving teachers it will not come at all. The hierarchy of the profession needs to be broken down from within by establishing new lines of communication and association not only between schools, but between schools, colleges and universities.

Reference

1. Konrad Lorenz, *On Aggression* (Methuen 1966; Harcourt Brace Jovanovich, 1966).

CHAPTER 8
Resources for Learning

In the instructional school governed by streaming, class grouping and the timetable, the question of providing resources for learning is simple. If you have enough money, you have enough books and enough laboratory equipment for a definite series of nonexperiments (i.e., doing what the book says to get the results it predicts), and you have enough machinery to make the particular engineering products from which we can learn engineering. Since the only product ever examined is information bundled in an approved fashion and quantity the logistics are simple—have enough sources for the information you want to get back. The centre of all learning is the textbook, or whatever else does in another medium what the textbook does in print.

Obviously this conveniently simple but naive approach will not work for the kind of learning I have been advocating. It wouldn't even do to go for a much greater multimedia collection of materials devised with a deliberately instructional intention. You can have too much of a good thing. Information too readily discovered devalues the searching which is learning. Learning is much more seeking than getting, much more experience than information.

Not even a perfect collection of learning games with clues to action guaranteeing the experience from which we can learn would do. To rely on *any* collection is to claim to have predicted all the learning that needs to be done. And we are in no position to make such predictions. In any case if we overpredict we leave ourselves at the mercy of unpredicted changes; we eliminate the flexibility of response to the unexpected which is our most valuable talent. Even if we could compose games allowing for unpredictable results (which is technically possible but horribly difficult to do) we would still be robbing the learner of exercise in collaborative invention, of chasing hares which just cropped up and weren't released from a trap for coursing.

To think in terms of providing all that is needed for learning carefully chosen and parcelled rather than determining to explore collaboratively anything that can be discovered in our world and in ourselves is to manipulate and play Pygmalion—as faulty and hostile a decision as the decision to play Procrustes. So it seems to me that most valuable of all resources for learning—and the least exploited—is our capacity for collaboration. Wherever the young see us trying to canalize the direction of their thoughts in a direction they weren't about to take, they reject us and quite rightly:

> The kind of games teachers make us play are usually just boring drill . . . . For instance, one of the schoolteacher's favourites is the silence game. The whole class sits as still as possible and the teacher calls up whoever's quietest, and he goes and stands by the blackboard and looks carefully round the class at the rest of them and see who's quietest, and writes his name on the board; and then *he* comes up to the board and the first one goes and sits in the second one's place and so on. But this so called game isn't a game at all—it's just a trick to keep us all quiet when the teacher wants to read the paper. They play this game in all the elementary classes here, and the daft thing is, most of the kids like it.[1]

Nor is the game in which all the relevant information about a farm is provided and you pretend to be a farmer, making decisions of a predetermined kind, a game. It is a piece of programmed teaching, involving minimal role playing. I have already pointed out the dangers of role playing for ourselves in becoming teachers. It is a good resource for learning within limits given that we are allowed to play selfinvented roles as well as given ones and are allowed free dramatic improvisation as well as being called on to play Nasser in a game of Nations or customer in a game of Shop.

If we think that learning is the product of teaching, or that learning is mostly a matter of being instructed, we think we can help it by providing materials. If we think there is more to learning than that, we have to think more of discovering than of providing. In a fourfold curriculum the only process that can be thoroughly planned to use predetermined materials is the courses of autonomous study, and these in fact demand much more rigorously careful programming than we are accustomed to give to preparing lessons. In fact we could well commission much of what we need for such courses from professional programmers, supplementing them and adapting them for our local needs.

For the rest let us use the world as we find it and wish to transform it; let us not interpose ourselves between the young and the world, but look into it together. Energetic learning needs very little teacher direction. It goes best in fact if each party coopts the other into learning by the discovery of common interests. If we seek to collaborate genuinely in this discovery we cannot predict and prepare the materials we shall need. To do so we need to know beforehand at least what topics we shall be taking up. I think we have to develop a new view of the world itself and our social system as our resources for learning and begin to explore the viability of community itself as the educational medium.

In the instructional school there is a clear hierarchy of resources which reads:

1. Teachers who can give information verbally and graphically, and get some version of it back.

2. Books as stores of information; notebooks as personal containers.
3. Other media used like books to obtain information usually in the way appropriate to the medium, but given back as written notes.
4. Hardware for other media (tape recorders, film, and slide projectors, video equipment, maybe computers) and other hardware for predetermined exercises (gymnasium, workshop, labs and so on).
5. A physical envelope to contain these prescribed activities in separate compartments for class sized groups.
6. Decisions about what is to be learned (or rather, what is to be taught) entirely dominated by this hierarchy of resources expressed as timetable and syllabus.

This isn't even a pint pot for the ocean of urgently relevant information available for consideration. It is a selfcontained information system of a totally different kind from the information world in which we really live. It does not verify, it falsifies. It could be appropriate only to a world in which significant events of a kind which radically alter people's daily lives happen only rarely. It prepares people for such a life and makes them see life as being like that—slow, unlikely to be interrupted. It is a picture of a stable orderly world nailed over all the windows through which we would see, if we could look, a world in crisis which demands our urgent attention, where such things happen every day as demand that we join our efforts in the invention of some new means of control of events. With such a system we teach a dumb respect for cleverness, especially technological cleverness, while it threatens to destroy us—not some future generation, but *us* alive now.

The real world is *not* in order; it is in chaos. And it is in chaos because of the respect we are teaching for the old order of *laissez faire* and for science, because our educational system is still an obstacle race designed to maintain a selective recruitment to power of fairly docile clever hacks, because it systematically alienates by making us not care about what is happening as well as by dividing us into specialist groups each with its own kind of information to deal with.

Unless we both explore the real information world (the one in which events happen rapidly) and somehow intervene in the real social world together, we must go on falsifying. To gather information about past wars—even one as recent as that in which I grew up—and discuss values on the basis of that is an act of falsification, since neither the cause nor the conduct of war is as it was, nor is the condition of respect for human life so healthy.

I have for the past nine weeks been very much preoccupied with writing this book and have not kept an eye on the news. But in that time I know that the following things have happened. I list them at random:

1. New military governments have taken power in Algeria and Brazil. The Algerian revolution alters the balance of power in the Middle East again and may affect fuel supplies. The tentative movements towards greater freedom of thought in Czechoslovakia have been finally halted. Uncle Ho has died.
2. Men have landed and walked on the moon and we have better pictures of Mars.
3. Australian biologists have become worried about some ecological disturbance which is producing much greater numbers of a poisonous, tiny blue-ringed octopus.
4. Lobbying has started in earnest for a plan to dam the Amazon and produce a new vast inland sea—a project to provide one third of the present electric power supply of the USA at the certain cost of wiping out all remaining primitive amero-indians, and unpredictable but certainly great ecological disturbance.
5. Nail biting has been identified as the variable distinguishing between people who go on working with minor illnesses (biters) and those who take time off to get well (nonbiters).
6. Two simultaneously published US military documents have praised chemical and biological warfare research for bringing "vast and complex advantages in health, economics, and social betterment to the entire nation" (*The Army Digest*) and revealed what the research has shown as a result of

trials in Vietnam, listing new standard weaponry (Manual TC-3-16).

7. Belgian scientists have announced their success in getting bacterial DNA to join up with plant DNA, achieving a true genetic transplant which is in effect mating germs and plants.

8. Atomic explosion is to be used to decongest oil bearing seams. The oil will be radioactive but it will be marketed. The local effect will be that of a major earthquake so the population has to be moved out.

9. A number of deaths have resulted from injuries caused by wearing safety belts to prevent injury in car crashes.

10. A system of computer matching of tissues has been set up in London to speed up the development of an organ bank for transplant operations.

11. A complicated plan has been proposed for taxing all traffic moving through central London.

Eleven random items of news from two momths. So what? There were undoubtedly many more and some of them undoubtedly of greater significance. But this world is clearly *not* the information world of instructional schools, and why are these resources being excluded?

Because they are news; they cannot be planned; the handling of them cannot be predetermined; they aren't questions and there aren't any answers. Yet awareness of such events is the only possible basis for the kinds of decision we all need to share in making.

They are decisions of this kind:

If someone were to ask us to state openly whether we were for or against certain kinds of progress—and the problem arises at the moment with the development of atomic energy—it is at least conceivable that a large number of people might say "No, it would be better not to have that, it would be better to stay as we are." The fact of owning a car does not seem to me to be an advantage in itself; it is an indispensable form of defence in a society in which many other people have cars; but if I could choose, and if all my contemporaries would agree to give up their cars too, I would drive mine to the scrap heap with great relief.[2]

That was Lévi-Strauss talking ten years ago. Only ten years. What has happened since has made the power of atomic energy the least of our worries—much greater powers have since been invented.

Two years ago Gordon Rattray Taylor settled down to write a book reviewing recent developments in biotechnology. It took a year to write. When finished, he had to add a stop press comment on developments so recent he could not explore them in the book:

> Since I drafted this book events have moved rapidly. The transplantation of hearts has been in the head-lines . . . . Anxiety has been found to have a chemical basis bringing mood control a big step nearer. An effective genetic viral code (DNA) has been synthesized, making the manufacture of new manmade viruses an immediate possibility. Scientists . . . have shown that the selfassembling tendency of chemical units goes even further than was thought, each amino acid unit having a preference for association with certain others. Most significant of all, the process of "cloning" has been extended from the order of plants known as dicotyledons to the monocots, by the cloning of asparagus, thus lending weight to the belief that it can be carried out with any type of cell.
>
> All this (and more) is less than twelve months: what will the next twelve years bring?[3]

I will not reproduce here his three-phase list of imminent developments. It includes by 1975 artificial viruses, mind modifying drugs and extensive power to postpone clinical death by keeping organs going in a kind of human cabbage patch until somebody else needs them; by 2000, extensive mind modification and personality reconstruction, reconstructed organisms, the first cloned animals (cloning is reproduction without mating, inducing cells of a parent to develop an exact reproduction) and man/animal chimeras. Shortly after 2000 he expects an extension of the life-span by up to fifty years, disembodied brains, cloned people and man/machine chimeras.

His book was written to warn not of what will happen soon, but of what happens now, what has already happened to increase powers nobody is trying to control:

> While a few imaginative scientists have been trying to consider the implications of their work, the majority never do so, but just carry on from day to day with the problem in hand, recking as little of the wider issues as a bank clerk does of monetary policy.[4]

Can alienation go further yet than this? Have we not reached the end of the road? An item from my news list I left out was this:

12. Two thieves, a man and a woman, after robbing a man they met outside a pub, tied him by the foot to the railway line in the path of an oncoming express which cut his foot off. They saw it coming but walked hurriedly away. Perhaps they preferred knowing what was going to happen to actually seeing it.

But our young need to see what is happening in the world and if they can convert their vision into questions for which they can find any sort of answer we should welcome those answers with relief. For we, so far, have miserably failed.

All this may seem a roundabout way of making the point that whatever we do about resources we should not interpose a distorting filter between the world and ourselves. For resourcing interdisciplinary enquiry the answer is simple—plan as little as possible. Rely on a strength you are not used to using, the collective strength of the diversity of insights and ingenuities which already exists in the group of clusters and focus group. Use all the normal media and invent experiments. Don't look at all towards special filtered information designed to instruct. For resources in the other processes use what you have to begin with but extend your use of media by adopting the response best for each—answer a film with a film, a play with a play, a diagram with a diagram. Don't make the media act like books. Don't make reading and writing hack activities and so destroy them. Have only what is worth writing written and only what is worth reading read. Learn to program where you clearly mean to instruct. Where any machinery is provided, let the young use it to make what they themselves have designed and not more obsolete lumber. In the science laboratories encourage experiments rather than nonexperiments.

But above all free the young to use the world and be prepared to learn from them as well as with them. Your acceptance is the most important of all their resources for learning. It isn't a matter of changing our minds but of seeing how our minds have been changed:

> Our minds are already changed . . . what remains to be done is to find out what tools are at our disposal and how to use them so that our objective is never seen in the distance but rests continually inside each one of us . . . .
> They speak of evolution. Where is there a sense of proportion? Talk, talk, talk: is that what we must put up with? . . . . How in heaven's name did anyone get the idea that proportion took place in an object outside of him? A little flexibility of mind and one is able to use it wherever he looks . . . . Not the perceptions of the proportions of things outside of us (this is obviously a physical impossibility; that's why it's a mental responsibility) . . . . Conversation should be more affluent, each remark unfolding unsuspected ideas and terms of thought. Where our sense of proportion was violated, it no longer is, just as the most common variety of anything is nowadays a rare experience. We still have a few prejudices hanging around and even if we don't remove them ourselves dear friends come in and do it for us.[5]

If we can open ourselves to each other that is. We can see the world we live in only with each other's personal and unique help. It is not a foreknown world but strange to all of us and frightening.

One last comment I shall make but not pursue. What I have been describing in this book as a fourfold curriculum is not a school but a system of education which can be applied to schools. It would work just as well and maybe better without schools at all, but with small adolescent meeting places instead to be used as bases for exploration of the world, places in which to play, work out enquiries and hold exhibitions. Instruction and experience could be got elsewhere, along with adults who are learning or relearning. Before long we shall all be students most of the time. Why develop two separate systems?

Summary

1. Planned publication of resource materials simply cannot cope with the speed of events that the young should consider. We should encourage them to use ordinary public media and explore the world opportunistically.
2. We should promote the *use* of far more media by the young rather than using them simply as sources of information.
3. Equipment should be used more for invention than for instruction.
4. Where there is a clear intention to instruct, the instruction should be well programmed to achieve short-term objectives.
5. The most important resources are personal and are to be found in the collective insights of the collaborative group of teachers and youngsters, given that they relate authentically.

References

1. Danilo Dolci, *For the Young* (MacGibbon and Kee, 1967).
2. Claude Lévi-Strauss, in G. Charbonnier, *Conversations with Claude Lévi-Strauss* (Cape Editions, 1969; Grossman, 1969).
3. G. Rattray Taylor, *The Biological Time Bomb* (Thames and Hudson, 1968; New American Library, 1969).
4. See note 3 above.
5. John Cage, "Rhythm etc," in *Module, Symmetry, Proportion*, Gyorgy Kepes, ed. (Studio Vista, 1966).

Afterword

Although I believe the critique and the recommendations I make in this book apply wherever teachers undertake to educate adolescents, I wrote it first for British teachers and parents, assuming a knowledge of the secondary school system in which they work or see their children taught.

Now that it appears in an American edition I have to clarify my description of our schools so that American readers can compare them with their own and judge for themselves the relevance of my book to their own young. The ideas in it have been discussed with teachers from most parts of the world, so I am assured it's no impertinence to offer it abroad: most adults in most nations feel that there's some problem in their relationship with the young, and that's the central theme of the book.

I have deliberately adopted a polemical approach, hoping to provoke readers into looking afresh at a system so familiar to them it may have turned into a sacred cow. The notion that we have a right to compel youngsters to attend classes in schools, and can discharge in that way our obligation to offer them an education, is entrenched as deeply in "democratic" as it is in "totalitarian" societies. That notion I find it necessary to challenge. An English reviewer suggested that I believe education does the young more harm than good. I don't; but I do believe the kind of secondary schools we have are severely damaging to all who work in them, young and old alike, and that their incompatibility with democratic ideals is one of the strongest forces preventing the achievement of democracy in our "advanced" societies. I don't expect those who do not share my attachment to democracy to be converted by this book; at most I hope to force those who talk democratic and act otherwise to reexamine their position.

Until as recently as the 1944 Education Act the undemocratic nature of the British educational system was obvious even in Britain. It was of course more widespread than a national system has a right to be, since it was also a model serving much of the world, for the empire we have since fortunately lost also adopted it, and the neocolonial states carved out of the empire have retained its pattern, just as the equally academic and elitist French system still dominates much of Africa.

Since shortly after the war of 1939-45 ended (and those years of public profession of democratic principles certainly affected the 1944 Act) the main innovation in Britain has been the extension of secondary education, which used to be the privilege of a minority, to everybody up to the age of 15 (the target of 16 having been deferred till the country can afford it, a time now expected to arrive in 1973). What is actually offered as secondary education (universal) is strangely like what used to be offered as secondary education (suitable for bright kids only).

The basic offer now is six years of primary education plus four years of secondary in a different school. The base of the prewar system was nine years in the same elementary school, which children were compelled to attend until they reached the age of 14 unless their parents paid for them to attend a private school or they qualified in an examination at 11 for a free place in a grammar school, which only a minority did. This means that there are three possible sources of educational tradition

which could operate on the new universal secondary schools—
private schools, state-maintained day grammar schools, and
elementary schools.

Most private schools were (and are) overtly middle class in
values, retaining or seeking to emulate the traditions of our
oddly named Public Schools, mostly Victorian foundations,
outside the state system and identified closely with British
imperialism, their chief customers initially having been colonial
and military officers who needed boarding schools to park their
young in while they wandered abroad on their business of
conquering and governing and making commerce. Other children in these schools were those of parents who enjoyed
privilege at home, or aspired to do so. The Public Schools
proper eventually fixed their age of entry at 13. Younger
children intended for them were sent to preparatory schools till
ready, or prepared by tutors at home.

To the most powerful of these schools (where you could get
to know the friends you would later meet in Parliament) entry
was guaranteed only by birth; wealth alone was not enough, and
scholarships were available for the well born but impoverished
such as Kipling or George Orwell. Exit into a university, the
army or a profession was also guaranteed. Small wonder that
there were many inferior imitations, and that when the state
grammar schools developed they also offered the flattery of
imitation. Schooling was dominated by the classics (but with a
respect also for the physical sciences), and it was scholarly but
avoided that somewhat shameful attribute of "mere cleverness."
The swot was no more trusted then than the egghead is today.
Building Character was the most discussed aim, with the
disciplines of field games and paramilitary organizations as the
means. Character meant something different from the "well-
rounded personality" which is the fashion now. The relationship of such an education to *power* was not merely assumed, it
was explicitly recognised, as Ruth First observes in *The Barrel
of a Gun*:

> Britain's army of colonial administrators, inbred and
> insular, was commanded by a senior corps, recruited in its

later years from Britain's Public Schools by a man who has
been called "an unreconstructed Victorian gentleman."
This was Sir Roger Furse, who controlled appointments to
civil service posts for thirty-eight years, from 1910 to
1948 . . . Furse was searching for men with special quali-
ties of leadership. Such men, he was convinced, came
invariably from certain families and educational institutions . . . his quick eyes took in personal mannerisms.
Following an interview in 1911, he wrote that the
candidate was "tall, light-haired, slim but well built . . . a
good open face with a good deal of grit in it . . . a very
good athlete . . . brains I expect fair . . . really up to East
African standard." . . . An official enquiry in 1929 clearly
agreed with the Duke of Devonshire when he said: "The
code which must guide the administrator in the tropics is
to be found in no book of regulations. It demands that in
every circumstance and under all conditions he shall act in
accordance with the traditions of an English gentleman."
Sir Roger Furse was right. The show could not have been
run without the public schools.

It reads oddly today, when men disguise the imperialist
motive automatically; but I myself as an adolescent met
teachers who justified their demands for conformity on me in
just such naive terms. Fortunately in my school such teachers
were counterbalanced by others, just as within the private
sector of education, outside state provision, there has always
been a small minority tradition of progressive education.
A. S. Neill's experiments could not have flourished in a state
school. Nevertheless the traditions of most private schools are
those of an ascriptive society in which men (and nations) inherit
rank, wealth and power, and need an education designed to
teach them how to use these privileges. Their schools inevitably
express and promote, in their organization and in their daily
life, ascriptive values, making a hierarchy of age and rank and
muscle, formalizing it in captaincies of teams, clubs and classes,
and Houses, in prefectships and in patronage: the very language

is Roman—the Empire rebuilt in Macaulayan images (and he was himself the son of a British African colonist). America perhaps needs foresight here—having an empire, or an equally dominant influence on the world, can be as bad for the soul as it's good for the pocket—the satraps tend to bring boss-attitudes home with the spoils.

On the face of it, British society has since shifted ground to become an "achieving society" in which men get power by merit, by earning it somehow, not by inheritance; and, of course, on the face of it, American society has always been of that type, has never been ascriptive. I have my doubts in both cases: the persistence of ascriptive values in British schools is evident; and Ferdinand Lundberg in *The Rich and the Super-rich*, seems quite justified in his claim that inherited wealth confers great power on its owners in the United States, with privileges not a whit less fortified than those of our Victorian oligarchy were. The odd reality is that the *shape* of British schooling for adolescents is more like that of the Public Schools than it ever was before, not less. What has happened is that of the three available traditions the elitist models have coalesced, the alternative (elementary) model has been dismantled, and no genuine alternative has yet been shaped.

Before the advent of universal secondary education most people attended elementary schools from the age of 5 to 14. Some elementary schoolchildren, in proportions showing very great regional variations, but never topping one-fifth, were given "scholarships" for good grades in a public examination taken at 11 years old, enabling them to attend free (or at a reduced fee) state grammar schools, to the age of 16 in most cases. After five years they tackled a barrage of examinations (then called Lower Schools Certificate). If they did well, they might stay on for a further two years of more specialized study, preparing for a Higher School Certificate exam, which was the effective barrier of entry to university. This "scholarship route" was the "achieving" element in an otherwise entirely ascriptive system. Others who did not win scholarships could transfer to gram-mar-school at 11 if their parents paid the full fees. There were a few technical high schools parallel to grammar schools in status; and there were also some "central schools" which were "superior" elementary schools.

Others still of course might buy their education throughout and have no contact with state schools at any time.

Some grammar schools financed themselves by taking almost equal proportions of scholarship and fee-paying pupils; and the most prestigious of these, along with Public Schools, composed a sort of club: their heads belonged to the Headmaster's Conference (which still exists). "H.M.C." schools had the best liaison with the universities, and along with them and the Civil Service Commissioners they heavily influenced the structure and nature of the School Certificate examinations, which were administered by the universities.

This constellation of influence on public examinations explains the famous anomaly of British education—that its freedom from direct state control yet produces a marvelous sameness. The curriculum of every school is in theory the concern only of its teachers; yet although decision of what and how to teach is said to be free and local, there is a striking similarity both of curriculum and internal organization of schools throughout the whole country. Provision and control of schools is a local matter, power being in the hands not of an elected school board but of the officers of a Local Authority (a city, a very large borough, or a county) who are answerable to a committee of elected councillors. Thus the state has no direct control; but education is the country's costliest service, and the bulk of money for the most expensive items (buildings and teachers' pay) is provided from central government, so the Secretary of State has the whip hand in any negotiations he undertakes with Local Authorities, and can of course alter national standards by legislation. In practice this means that education is subject to political prejudice both at national and at local levels; and it is to these pressures, rather than to any clearly defined curriculum-making authority, that our teachers, when exercising their freedom to decide what to do in their schools, find themselves responding. The question automatically put (if never quite in these words) is "how far is it safe to depart from custom?"

It has gone almost unnoticed how rapidly the country did in fact move away from custom in destroying the alternative elementary-school tradition, in a transition from small to large schools. The postwar reorganization legislated them out of existence; most of them were small, within walking distance of home for all pupils, and divided into classes by age without any kind of streaming (ability grouping). The new pattern was one of primary schooling from ages 5 to 11, followed by schooling to 15 in a secondary school which might be one of three types—grammar or technical schools for the most able (about one-fifth of the 11-year-olds) and modern schools for the rest. What then happened quite quickly was that, with some very distinguished exceptions, modern schools tried to rectify their inferiority of status by imitating the grammar schools. When the Labour government abolished this tripartite system, insisting that Local Authorities combine their different types of secondary schools into comprehensive schools (a process now halted in mid-course in many areas that retain their grammar schools) secondary education had settled down into the old grammar-school pattern, with a diluted version of its curriculum and the whole of its organization—streaming, batteries of tests and exams and all, and all teaching by specialists.

Traditionally, the grammar school teacher was always a specialist; his primary task and concern was to teach his subject with university entrance in mind, even though only a minority of his students would in fact achieve that goal. On the other hand, the elementary school teacher was a class-teacher; he might do a little specialist work, but he had to be competent in all basic subjects and he taught them throughout the year to his own class, in which clever and dim children worked together, and he spent most of his time with them. He probably divided his day into parcels of subject-time, but he had ample elbow-room to manipulate the situation and employ such methods as he thought fit.

This description still applies, of course, to most of our

primary schools, though streaming came into fashion in them too as they grew larger and as they became dominated by the selection-tests that the tripartite system demanded for a sorting-out of all children at 11, purely on academic ability. This encouraged primary teachers to spot their potential grammar-schoolers as early as possible and accelerate their progress by grouping them together. A whole generation has now been handled in this way, having suffered the experience of formal competition from a very tender age, and most teachers seem to have forgotten that this was an innovation, a move away from custom—it has become the custom they cling to. And parents too are still prone to judge a primary school on its success in winning grammar-school places for its pupils. So the former minority-practice of dividing pupils into homogeneous groups, in terms only of crude distinctions of academic skill, not of humanity or maturity, has become almost universal in all schools; and I would argue that this means a major shift in the values teachers operate with. If you handle any group as homogeneous the last thing you look for is the diversity within it. Such a restricted focus of perception has grave implications for the whole society, for diversity is the well-spring of social health; it is indeed the tool of evolution itself. The smaller the reservoir of available differences, the less chance there is of successful adaptation. The dangers of the practice of homogeneous grouping have not gone unrecognized, and it is being quite rapidly eroded now in primary schools (some even managing not to revert to the old class-teaching pattern) but in secondary schools it is still deeply entrenched, and those which avoid it are clearly exceptional.

Against this background I can now sketch the probable educational career of a child in this country.

AGE 5. Begin full-time schooling in the infant department of a state primary school (or if parents wish and can afford it, a private school; many parents in fact use state primary schools and then pay for a private school from 11 onwards). A very few can prepare for this by going to nursery schools at 3; but there aren't many of them.

AGE 7. Enter the junior department of the same primary

school. (Unless it is one of those schools which organize on "family-grouping" rather than on age-equal classes; these are still relatively rare). The general social assurance of your family, in which wealth and job-security are important elements, will heavily influence your relationship with teachers and your consequent success in schoolwork. If your parents and your teachers just don't talk the same language, your chances are very slim indeed.

AGE 9 (in some areas of Britain only—a variant pattern). Transfer to another school, a middle school of children from 9 to 13 years. (But in a small number of other areas, this could be from 8 years to 12.) From a middle school you will transfer eventually to a high school, which will be organized like any secondary school. If you do go to a middle school, the chances are that it will be employing methods derived from experiments in primary education, and will be progressive.

AGE 11, in most Local Authorities. Transfer to a comprehensive school, if reorganization in your area has been completed and there are no remnants of the tripartite system left. If your area has upgraded all its modern schools to comprehensives, but still keeps grammar schools, you will face selection procedures to determine where you go. Or you may go either to a modern or a comprehensive or a grammar school. Since most comprehensive schools are in fact rigidly streamed, and it is quite common practice for the "bright" streams to be called grammar streams, you in fact face selection at 11 anyway, and may come to see your school simply as the tripartite system on one big campus.

Parental choice of school, as a matter of civil rights, is supposed to be very important at this stage. If your parents decide to leave you in the state system, your primary school head will forward test results and her own comments on you to the local Education Officer, who will in effect decide where you go. If your parents object he'll negotiate; usually you end up negotiated into the place decided for you to begin with. In urban areas where schools are thick on the ground the jockeying can be complicated, and your parents will be asked to name three schools in order of preference. The schools may well be of the same type but very differently esteemed by most parents, for very obvious reasons. Two schools in central London spring to my mind—one alongside a park, in a very rich housing district, quite spacious, with ambassadors' and Cabinet Ministers' children attending it, a comprehensive school visited day in, day out by parties of foreign educationists; another, still a comprehensive school, in walking distance, but over a main road and round a few back streets, a slum among slums. All the children in the fine school made it first choice. So did most of the children in the other; many of them in fact are in a school that didn't appear on their list of three at all. In such a case, the superior school is over-subscribed, and though it has to keep to the rules of maintaining a mixture on academic factors, within that pattern it selects the children of the most stable and ambitious families.

The differences in fact between neighboring schools of notionally equal status reflect simply the nuances of the English social-class system. One school will develop a large sixth-form and another will not because it has concentrated in it children who know at 11 that they're killing time till they can leave at 15; and their teachers will frankly refer to such schools as "rough" or "tough" or "dumps."

AGE 15. Leave and get a job, if there is one available, or stay at school to take a leaving-examination at 16 which will get you a better job, or stay on till after 16 to make sure of getting that certificate, or stay on till 18 to get a higher certificate which may get you into a university and earn a degree, or failing that (since we have only half the university places for people formally qualified to enter them) go into a College of Advanced Technology, where you can still earn a degree; or failing that, a College of Education, where you may be able to take a degree but in any case can qualify as a teacher, in which case . . .

AGE 21. Go back to school, this time for life.

So many variables in a state system of education superficially disarm criticism: it seems impossible to make valid generalizations about it. But when you come to look at our schools and the way they are run, you find there is very little diversity of ideology-in-action. The greatest range of diversity to be found here is in our primary schools. Many of them are still entirely formal on an old pattern, streamed in age-equal classes, each class belonging to a teacher who faces from her desk in front of the blackboard rows of restrained children sitting at desks. Not a few are quite open, without classrooms at all, children moving freely among well-equipped working areas and referring as they need to members of a team of teachers who work well together. Very many are working in one of the possible intermediate styles between these two extremes. In secondary schools of whatever type or status, although there is much debate and experiment going on, there is a clearly visible uniform pattern of organization, and the dominant ideal is still the grammar schools which, compromising between their ideal of the public schools and the different reality of day-education, established that kind of organization.

So much of this book is given to a criticism both of the underlying ideology of such schools and of its outward casing, the organizational practice, that I won't summarize it here. I want only to add some comments on a few points where the strongly national flavor of British education shows through, points I mention elsewhere without dwelling on them.

First: our schools still prefer children in uniform to children wearing what they please. The uniform is usually modeled on the House-games dress of Victorian public schools—blazer, flannels and a peaked cap of the kind worn by cricketers or rowers for boys, dark skirts and blouses for girls (who being pricklier about fashion have got rid of the serge hockey-tunic that used to be the grammar-schoolgirls' uniform.) Students are subjected to very great pressure to wear this rig. But only twenty years ago uniform was limited to "superior" schools and was visible evidence of privilege. The scramble for "parity of esteem" among the new secondary schools spread it like wildfire, and it has now crept down even to primary schools. I can't escape concluding that this phenomenon indicates something important about the *model* of "good education" the nation has in mind—both teachers who defend the practice with very great heat (perhaps because they realize surreptitiously that it is in fact an impertinence) and the parents who mostly readily assent to it. Local authorities even make uniform-grants to parents who find the cost a burden. What used to be quite overtly paramilitary aspects of Public Schools have disappeared; is this the form in which an old purpose has been petrified?

Second: most secondary schools have readily adopted—and adapted—a house system for the organization of some of the activities of the school. The origins of this structure also lie in grammar-school imitation of residential Public Schools, where houses had initially a very practical purpose. Teachers then took pupils into their own homes as lodgers—or rather supervised large lodging-houses apart from the school-buildings proper—so that the school was composed of such houses as genuine social units. The housemaster acted *in loco parentis*, and had a full-time job of overall care for the youngsters in his house. In the grammar schools, nonresidential of course, the housemaster took on only one part of this role, becoming a kind of disciplinary chieftain of a part-time tribe. A school of 600 would have probably four such houses, named for national worthies like Drake or Nelson, and the four housemasters would be teachers of high status, superior to heads of academic departments, and composing the inner council of the headmaster's lieutenants, through whose authority over both teachers and pupils the head effectively ran his school. The houses competed for trophies both in studies and in sports (which a generation ago were pursued with almost religious fervor). Through this house-system senior pupils also came to exercise power, as house prefects with the duty of policing their juniors and the right to punish them in a variety of ways which included beating.

This prefectorial system was adopted by most schools along with the rest of house-paraphernalia as universal secondary education spread (but not the power to beat: corporal punishment, which is still frequently used in some areas, is the prerogative of teachers). Very big comprehensive schools especially favor the house-system cross-hatching the academic system to express the dual purpose of the school—to care for as well as to teach. The house system is meant to counter the dangers of depersonalization in big institutions and to give teachers a paternal (or maybe an avuncular) role as well as an instructional one. I don't think the system succeeds in fact; indeed, I find it difficult to understand why children who have parents need a teacher to stand *in loco parentis* to them.

Teachers in our schools still tend to relate badly, or not at all, to parents. In spite of much official pressure (which is I think now beginning effectively to wear down the barriers) schools fight shy of Parent-Teacher Associations, preferring very formal contacts, inviting parents in only on "state occasions" or to complain about their children's misbehaviors. For this again there may be traditional causes. The grammar school tradition was one in which the parents were likely not to be able to understand in any detail the schooling their children were getting—the relationship was class-conscious. The parent was to be grateful for the opportunities his son or daughter was getting, and to relate to the school's head as he would to the gentry. The elementary schoolteacher was likely to teach the whole family anyway, to stay in the same place long enough to teach you and then your children, and really not to need formalities of contact. Both traditions contribute to the present reality, which is that the head teacher has almost total autocratic power over his school (if he chooses to use it that way) so long as he doesn't fall foul of his local Education Officer or Committee, as he would of course be likely to do if too many parents complained about his way of running things. Still, parents mostly don't complain. We are still in an early stage of the shift from education-as-a-privilege to education-as-a-right.

Finally in my short list of national peculiarities, I must explain the importance of sixth forms, the size of which is economically important to a secondary school as well as prestigious. It confers prestige because it indicates the academic quality of the school; in the past, only grammar schools had them, and they were not important simply as a senior class; the potential sixth-former was a favored pupil right through his school career. Most of our grammar schools were founded after local authorities were encouraged to develop them by the Act of 1902. At the time, elementary education was free and

compulsory, but you could leave (as my mother did) at 12 if
you had reached the nationally agreed standard. You could
transfer from your elementary school to a grammar school at 11
if you passed a Scholarship Examination, paying nothing, part
or full fees according to your parents' income. If you
transferred, you entered a five-year grammar-school course and
accepted an obligation to stay with it until you were 16, when
you would by examination earn a certificate which guaranteed
you a good job. At the height of British imperialist expansion-
ism, and even in its warm afterglow following the First World
War, this put the workingclass scholarship child on the crest of a
wave, along with the children of those who were rich enough to
buy such schooling anyway.

The grammar schools were clearly seen and acknowledged to
be making an elite. It was the highroad of social mobility for
clever children, and it was shaped to that end; for many it had
the groundswell of revolutionary possibilities, but for most it
meant escape from "the laboring classes" and entry into the
security of a profession (teaching itself becoming the goal for
many, coloring the profession still with ambivalence on the
social-class issue).

But out of this academic/social elite emerged another—those
who would stay at school beyond the five years, continuing
more specialist studies for a further two years to get entry to
the handful of English universities. The five-year course was
general—Divinity, English, Maths, History, Geography, one of
more of Languages and Sciences, and Classics, with some
element of narrow choice to express a humanities or sciences
bias. In the sixth form you became a specialist in two or three
subjects; and with good enthusiastic teachers it was possible to
get a deep enjoyment from your studies. My own debt to my
sixth-form teachers is one I'm happy to acknowledge.

The highest measure of worth grammar schools applied to
themselves was the number of places their sixth-formers won in
universities; it was the custom to keep a record of them
displayed on ornate plaques on the walls of the school hall.
Places won by the most esteemed means, the winning of a
university college scholarship, were nationally newsworthy, not

just in the educational press, but important enough to be published in *The Times*. I doubt whether any of us who saw our names printed in those lists (our schools printed after us in brackets) felt anything but pride and warmth at the time. Inevitably, there was keen competition among schools; the annual score was published—and the game still goes on. Inevitably, too, these were the ambitions dominating the lives of grammar-school teachers. As a pupil, you faced a battery of tests every term (we have three school terms a year) or maybe even at the end of every month, so that you always knew your current rating, and could rouse yourself for an all-out effort each summer, when the end-of-year examinations decided whether you held your place in your stream, or achieved promotion (if not already at the top) or disgraced yourself and went down to a lower form.

Life in the sixth form was more gracious. You didn't get there at all if you hadn't mastered the tactics by which examiners are defeated, and you no longer had to study subjects that didn't interest you. A genuine scholar now, you were free of the drudgery you had had to face in the years of arriving, and could forget the anxiety that the relentless competition had provoked. Most likely, just like the teachers running the system (with whom you now identified closely anyway) you no longer had any sharp sense left of the pains there had to be to make you into a winner, in thrall to the puritan ethic, to an expansionist ideology which preaches that all men can be winners if only they can be more like you, and to inflexibly narrow notions of human worth.

I'm indicating the kind of damage privilege does to the privileged. Unfortunately, although secondary education in Britain is now a universal right, it has retained the values of the selective system that preceded it, and the format of those values; the old inegalities are still buried in it, expressed in a preference for calm, conformist, scholarly man, rather than for the lively, the contented, the original or the plain pleasant ordinary human creature.

But there's a cash incentive too. A state school's finances, its staff salaries and staffing ratio are decided on a "points" system, and every sixth-former is worth multiple points, so that it is to a school's advantage in every way to persuade pupils to stay on, although that means that the sixth form must contain more purposes than its old one of polishing the elite. A growing recognition of the quaintness (to say the least) of applying the old means to young adults whose vision of ends may at no point match the old order is bringing changes about in this area rather more rapidly than in others. The exit is more likely to be rebuilt than the entrance, however lunatic it may seem to subject the young to an inappropriate and largely irrelevant circus of subjects and then hastily try to repair damage that need never have been done.

One of the values of history should be that we don't have to force each succeeding generation to recapitulate, before it frees itself, all those excursions up blind alleys that we took ourselves.

Bibliography

Particularly Important Books

Dolci, Danilo, *For the Young* (MacGibbon and Kee, 1967).
Doxiadis, Constantin, *Between Dystopia and Utopia* (Faber, 1968).
Durkheim, Emile, *Essays on Sociology and Philosophy* (Harper and Row, 1965).
James, Charity M., *Young Lives at Stake* (Collins, 1968; Agathon, 1971).
Kelly, G. A., *The Psychology of Personal Constructs* (Norton, 1955).
Lorenz, Konrad, *On Aggression* (Methuen, 1966; Harcourt Brace Jovanovich, 1966).
Mason, Edwin, *Starter Kits* (Ward Lock Educational, 1970).

Other Books

Bannister, D., and Mair, J. M. M., *The Evaluation of Personal Constructs* (Academic Press, 1968).

Collaborative Learning

Barnes, D. R., "Language in the Secondary Classroom," in *Language, the Learner and the School* (Penguin, 1969).

Becker, Ernest, *The Birth and Death of Meaning* (Free Press of Glencoe, 1962; Collier, 1963).

Blishen, Edward, *The School That I'd Like* (Penguin, 1969).

Blythe, Ronald, *Akenfield* (Allen Lane, The Penguin Press, 1969; Pantheon, 1970).

Bowker, Gordon, *Education of Coloured Immigrants* (Longmans Green, 1968; Humanities Press, 1969).

Britton James, "Talking to Learn," in *Language, the Learner and the School* (Penguin, 1969).

Bruner, Jerome, *Toward a Theory of Instruction* (Harvard University Press, 1966; OUP 1966).

Cage, John, "Rhythm etc.," in *Module, Symmetry, Proportion*, Gyorgy Kepes, ed. (Studio Vista, 1966).

Charbonnier, G., *Conversations with Claude Lévi-Strauss* (Cape Editions, 1969; Grossman, 1969).

De Bono, E., *The Use of Lateral Thinking* (Cape, 1967; Basic Books, 1968).

Drucker, Peter F., "The Knowledge Society," in *New Society* (August 24, 1969).

Dyckman, John W., "Some Conditions of Order in an Urbanized World," in *Daedalus* (summer 1966).

Enright, D. J., *The Old Adam* (Hogarth Press, 1965; Wesleyan University Press, 1965).

Eysenck, H. J., "Behaviour Therapy Versus Psychotherapy," in *New Society* (August 7, 1969).

Freud, Sigmund, *Civilization and Its Discontents* (Hogarth Press, 1930; Norton, 1962).

Gordon, W. J., *Synectics* (Harper and Row, 1961).

Henry, Jules, "Social and Psychological Preparations for War," in *The Dialectics of Liberation*, David Cooper, ed. (Penguin, 1968).

Hudson, Liam, *Frames of Mind* (Methuen, 1968).

Kozol, Jonathan, *Death at an Early Age* (Houghton Mifflin, 1967; Penguin, 1968).

Laing, R. D., "The Obvious," in *The Dialectics of Liberation*, David Cooper, ed. (Penguin, 1968).

Bibliography

Lambert Royston, *The Hothouse Society* (Weidenfeld and Nicolson, 1969).

Leavis, F. R., *The Common Pursuit* (Chatto and Windus, 1952).

Mays, J. B., *The Young Pretenders* (Michael Joseph, 1965; Schocken, 1968).

Mead, Margaret, in *Time* (September 4, 1954).

Nichols, Theo, "The Sociology Game," in *New Society* (July 1, 1969).

Ottaway, A. K. C. ,*Learning Through Group Experience* (Routledge, 1966; Humanities Press, 1966).

Piaget, Jean, *Six Psychological Studies* (LUP, 1968; Random House, 1968).

Sampson, Anthony, *Anatomy of Britain Today* (Hodder and Stoughton, 1965; Harper and Row, 1966).

Sargant, William, "The Physiology of Faith," in *New Society* (July 17, 1969).

Smith, L. A., in *The Raising of the School Leaving Age*, Pilot Course Report (Goldsmiths' College, 1966).

Stenhouse, Laurence, "Open Minded Teaching," in *New Society* (July 24, 1969).

Taylor, G. Rattray, *The Biological Time Bomb* (Thames and Hudson, 1968; New American Library, 1969).

Taylor, Calvin, and Warren, Frank, *Scientific Creativity* (John Wiley, 1963).

Taylor, Ian, "Hooligans: Soccer's Resistance Movement," in *New Society* (August 17, 1969).

Waddington, C. H., "The Modular Principle and Biological Form," in *Module, Symmetry, Proportion*, Gyorgy Kepes, ed. (Studio Vista, 1966).

Warren, Neil D., "Who Are the Backward?" in *New Society* (August 28, 1969).

Wiener, Norbert, *The Human Use of Human Beings* (Houghton Mifflin, 1954; Sphere Books, 1968).

Willmot, Peter, *Adolescent Boys in East London* (Routledge, 1966; Humanities Press, 1966).

Index

Index

Keller, Helen, 96
Kelly, G. A., 12, 28, 91, 97, 106
Kohl, Herbert, 4
Kozol, Jonathan, 63, 83

Laing, R. D. 47, 53
Lambert, Royston, 121, 146
Language, 97
  erosion, 45
Learning, 183 ff.
  process, 30, 72, 92-93
  subject matter, 147 ff.
Leavis, F. R., 21, 22, 28
Leonard, George, 4
Lévi-Strauss, Claude, 58, 83, 188, 192
Lindbeck, John, 139
Literature, 154
Lorenz, Konrad, 175, 182
"Loss of self," 42
Lower Schools Certificate, 197
Lundberg, Ferdinand, 197
Lynd, Staughton, 7

Manipulation, 172
Marcuse, Herbert, 45
Marin, Peter, 4
Marriage, 61, 65, 68
Mauger, Sam, 26, 139
Mays, J. B., 18, 28
McLuhan, Marshall, 43
Mead, Margaret, 41, 52
Michael, Lloyd, 5
Montgomery County (Md.) Student Alliance, 2

Neill, A. S., 196
Nichols, Theo, 33, 52

Organization, 163
Ottaway, A. K. C., 25, 28

Piaget, Jean, 124, 125, 146
Postman, Neil, 4
Poverty studies, 156
Power, 38, 172
Prefectorial system, 204
Primitive society, 58
Private schools, 195
Projects, 137 ff.
Public Schools, 195

Reciprocity, 114
Remedial studies, 116, 158 ff.
Retardation, 159
Role playing, 177, 178

Sampson, Anthony, 87, 106, 108, 117
Sand, Ole, 5
Sargant, William, 110, 118
Scholarships, 197
Schooling, in England, by age, 200
Schools, redesign of, 131-132
"Schools without walls," 5
Science, vs. art, 34
Security, 77
Sexuality, 61, 65, 68, 78
Silberman, Charles, 5
Simulations, 139
Sixth forms, 205
Smith, Leslie, 26, 112, 129, 139, 146
Social systems, 92
Special interest studies, 117, 161 ff.
Specialist teachers, 72
Standardization, 60

Index